DELULU IS NOT THE SOLULU

DELULU IS ^NOT THE SOLULU

The Secret to Staying Sane While Falling Apart

NATASHJA RATHORE

HAY HOUSE

HAY HOUSE INDIA
New Delhi • London • Sydney
Carlsbad, California • New York City

Hay House Publishers (India) Pvt Ltd
Muskaan Complex, Plot No. 3, B-2, Vasant Kunj, New Delhi – 110070, India

Hay House LLC, P.O. Box 5100, Carlsbad, CA 92018-5100, USA
Hay House UK Ltd, 1st Floor, Crawford Corner, 91-93 Baker Street, London W1U 6QQ, UK
Hay House Australia Publishing Pty Ltd, 18/36 Ralph St., Alexandria NSW 2015, Australia

Email: contact@hayhouse.co.in
Website: www.hayhouse.co.in

First published by Hay House India, 2026
Reprint, 2026
11 10 9 8 7 6 5 4 3 2

ISBN 978-93-6611-796-6 (Paperback)
ISBN 978-93-6611-237-4 (Ebook)

Printed at Thomson Press India Private Limited

FSC
www.fsc.org
MIX
Paper | Supporting responsible forestry
FSC® C010615

Hay House is committed to a sustainable future for our business, our readers and our planet. This book is made from Forest Stewardship Council® certified paper.

CONTENTS

Preface 11

Delulu 1: Delulu Is the Solulu **15**
Standard Issue 16
Assembly Line Rejects 17
Viral Defect 19
The Original Blueprint 21
Manufactured Reality 23
Packaging 25
Quality Control 27
Surveillance Room 30
Solulu 1: Face Your Triggers 33

Delulu 2: The Intellectual Is Intelligent **35**
Orientation Day 36
Class Teacher 37
Sacred Curriculum 39
Mass Indoctrination 41
Mental Detention 43
Theory of Knowledge 45
Class Topper 48
Solulu 2: Accept Appearing Foolish 51

Delulu 3: My Belief Is the Truth **53**
The Bubble of Belief 54
Believing to Seeking 56
Dispeller of Darkness 59
Science of Spirituality 61
Holy Trinity 63
Sounds as Keys 65
Ingredients of Creation 66

Temples as Technology 68
The Infinite Void 70
Solulu 3: Make Peace with Uncertainty 73

Delulu 4: I Am a Good Person 75
Lack OSX 76
Core Memory 78
Shameware 81
Performance Mode: On 84
Spiritual Firewall 86
Human_Behaviour.exe 89
Subconscious_Script.bat 91
Identity_Crash.log 93
Manual Override 95
System Reset 97
Solulu 4: Be Shamelessly Real 100

Delulu 5: Love Is Blind 103
The Love Drug 104
Cupid's Arrow 105
Those Three Words 108
Chasing Butterflies 109
The G(od) Spot 111
Trigger Me Tender 113
The Body Remembers 116
Runner & Chaser 118
Karmic Knots 120
Wishes & Dreams 122
Love Is God 125
Solulu 5: Commit to Love 128

Delulu 6: I Am Somebody 131
Role Play 132
The Imposter's Stage 134
The Opening Act 136
Dress Rehearsal 141
Break-a-Leg 144

Behind the Character 147
The Dance of Duality 150
The Final Solo 152
Solulu 6: Surrender to Insignificance 155

Delulu 7: Life Is Unfair 157

Charges Filed 158
Summons Served 159
Exhibit A: Loss 162
Cross-Examination 164
The Karma Dossier 166
Proceedings 169
The Witness 171
Preliminary Hearing 174
Continued Hearing 177
Final Verdict 180
Case Dismissed 182
Solulu 7: Assume All Responsibility 185

Delulu 8: I Will Change the World 187

The Saviour Complex 188
Codependency Counselling 190
Ancestral Untangling 192
The Doorway of Death 194
The Mechanics of Life 197
Smoke & Mirrors 199
The Sword of Clarity 202
Detachment 101 205
Natural Selection 2.0 208
Divine Duty 211
Mukti: The Ultimate Liberation 213
Solulu 8: Save Yourself First 218

Epilogue 221

Acknowledgements 227

ॐ असतो मा सद्गमय ।
तमसो मा ज्योतिर्गमय ।
मृत्योर्मा अमृतं गमय ।
ॐ शान्तिः शान्तिः शान्तिः ॥

Aum Asato-mā Sad-Gamaya
Tamaso-mā Jyotir-Gamaya
Mrityor-mā Amritam-Gamaya
Aum Shānti Shānti Shāntihi

Aum Lead me from Untruth to Truth
Lead me from Darkness to Light
Lead me from Mortality to Ultimate Liberation
Aum Peace Peace Peace

PREFACE

'People feel offended when I say
that the whole of humanity is insane,
but what can I do? It is so.'

- Osho

Let us begin with the elephant in the room—the silent but fabulous *J* in my name.

For the first twenty-three years of my life, I was Natasha, a name that obeyed all the phonetic rules. One day, my mother woke up, stared at the ceiling, and decided that numerology was the answer to all of life's problems. She insisted I add an extra A or S in the hope of a brighter future. This was hilarious, considering I already had more *Aas* and *Asha* than a Bollywood film. Both, by the way, mean 'hope' in Hindi.

Naturally, I protested. I was a staunch rationalist at the time, the type who rolled her eyes so hard they nearly dislocated. I hurt her feelings, and of course, felt guilty right after. So, I offered a compromise: I'd add a letter, provided I could choose another one to adopt.

Her eyes sparkled. 'J', she declared with divine conviction. Then she frowned, realising the J served absolutely no purpose. I didn't care. I was in love with the delicious absurdity of it all. A silent J. Like jalapeño. Sexy, confusing, mysterious, and pointless—just like me. So, I became 'Natashja'. It's been over ten years now, and honestly, I can't imagine my name without it.

As for the 'brighter future'—well, that depends on your definition of 'bright'. If you mean financial opulence, then no. I'm not there yet. I live in a rented apartment in a sleepy suburb of Coimbatore, because even the last crusty corner of Mumbai I once lived in is now a luxury item. I drive a gifted Suzuki Swift, work on a second-hand MacBook Pro, and earn just enough to avoid the tax department's radar.

And yet, I feel rich. Filthy rich.

My bills get paid. Work shows up when it has something interesting to say. I'm perpetually globetrotting. I live in an apartment kissed by a panoramic view of the Velliangiri Mountains and bathed in sunset light. I eat avocado toast and sip ABC juice like it's holy nectar. I even have a bunch of those ridiculously healing friends who always show up for me.

And when money runs low, the universe coughs up cash like a reliable sugar daddy.

I once bought an air conditioner for the guest room—Rs 45,000 I didn't have. I put it on my credit card, trusted the universe, and prayed I wouldn't have to sell my organs. The next day, a TDS refund of forty-six thousand landed in my account. Coincidence? Possibly. Divine comedy? Most definitely.

Another time, I spent a whole hundred thousand rupees flying to Prague for a wedding. Two days later—on Diwali night, no less—I received one and a half back from a five-year-old loan I'd emotionally buried and forgotten. At this point, I've stopped questioning it. The money comes. Always just enough to cover what I truly need for my well-being.

My current situation is such that I have no debt. I work from home with four cats, a collection of thriving houseplants, and no more romantic chaos. My mind is calm, my body strong, and my nervous system officially retired from drama. I've never had a cavity or sugar problem despite decades of shameless chocolate abuse. Other than the occasional vitamin deficiency, I've zero physical health issues—not even a pair of spectacles. I sleep well, have fun, and I'm, to put it simply, vibing.

But this doesn't mean my life is perfect. Life is still chaotic—but I'm not. I still get the occasional low, a necessary funeral for some illusion I've been clutching too tightly. But they're no longer collapse points.

It's important to mention, though, that it wasn't always like this.

I've been broke, heartbroken, injured, sick, and burnt out. I've seen the bottom. I've danced with depression, anxiety, and suicidal ideation. I've screamed into pillows and pleaded with the universe to make it stop. I've faced physical, emotional, psychological, and sexual violence. I've seen toxic relationships, health problems, workplace abuse, family chaos, betrayal, addiction, grief, and long stretches of 'what the actual hell is going on'.

And after everything I've been through, you'd think I'd at least get a little mental health disorder on paper; a little PTSD, if nothing. Nope. Turns out I'm officially sane.

Before putting this book out, I went through an exhaustive psychological evaluation at one of India's leading medical institutes. Apparently, my psychological profile is so flat it could double as a dosa. My reports literally read: 'Flat and non-pathological.'

The irony? The book was originally titled *Delulu Is the Solulu* because, honestly, I was expecting at least a dash of 'narcissistic artistic genius' or 'bipolar but lovable recluse'. After my diagnosis, I had to add the 'not'. Because how could I call myself 'delulu' after science declared me 'clinically boring'?

Perhaps that's the point. This book isn't born from an unending state of bliss or a complete mental breakdown. It's born from the messy middle, where life can still sucker punch you, but you don't lose yourself in the freefall. Where you're calm in the storm—not because the storm stopped, but because you finally realised you're not made of cardboard.

For most of my life, I thought spirituality was a scam. So, I set out to disprove it. Over the last fifteen years, the universe smirked and showed me the exact opposite. I've died a thousand small deaths, shed skins I didn't know I had, and quietly, stubbornly, become more me. Eventually, I learnt that 'bright' is merely a perspective. And when your perspective shifts, destiny shifts with it.

This book is not a spiritual guide. It's a hot mess of insights, cosmic truths, personal chaos, and laughter. Some of it may sound familiar. Some of it might make you throw the book across the room. But even if one sentence cracks open a space inside you, then I've done my job.

From one glorious, sacred delulu to another, I offer you this. May it remind you that your madness is not a malfunction. It's a portal.

With love, light, and unapologetic weirdness,
Natashja

Delulu 1

DELULU IS THE SOLULU

'If you are always trying to be normal, you will never know how amazing you can be.'

– Maya Angelou

STANDARD ISSUE

'Normal'—that elusive term we toss around like confetti at a parade, yet struggle to define. But what, pray tell, constitutes a 'normal' life anyway? Is it a stable job, two children, and a simmering undercurrent of marital resentment? Or maybe it's just being able to eat gluten without our digestive system filing a protest?

It seems most of us are flung into this world by parents eager to please their parents, extend the family tree, or dodge their own crushing loneliness. Some poor souls are even conceived as last-ditch attempts to slap a Band-Aid on a crumbling marriage.

Then comes school, where we spend years learning how to calculate the surface area of a cone but absolutely nothing about how to handle heartbreak, process shame, or stop spiralling at 2 a.m. because our crush left us on read. The education system really said: 'Here's algebra and the life cycle of a frog—good luck with taxes and existential dread!'

School doesn't teach us how to be ourselves. It teaches us how to blend in. Be smart, but not too smart. Funny, but only in socially approved doses. Pretty, but never prettier than the popular girl. It's a masterclass in becoming a bland biscuit of a human. Step one: Dilute yourself. Step two: Repeat until invisible.

If we stray too far from the norm, Congratulations! You're now 'the weird one'. Once that label sticks, it becomes our social identity, whether we like it or not.

Then we grow up and realise adult life is just school with bills and taxes. We chase jobs, promotions, pay cheques, and compliments like our souls depend on it. We scroll through other people's curated highlight reels and compare them to our behind-the-scenes bloopers. And somehow, we always feel like we're falling short.

And then there's love—the holy grail of validation and the lifelong audition for the role of 'Most Lovable Human'. We contort ourselves into emotional origami, hoping someone will pick us. We hand out parts of ourselves like free samples at a grocery store, praying someone takes the full-sized version home. Spoiler: They usually don't.

We eventually end up broken-hearted and blame everything. The system, our childhood, the patriarchy, mercury retrograde, even that chain e-mail we ignored in 2006. Anything but the real culprit: Our delusion that we have to become lovable rather than just be authentic.

I've been there. I've done the normal thing. Got the sticker marked 'weirdo' slapped on my forehead anyway.

Growing up was a wild patchwork. Born in Singapore but never quite Singaporean enough. Shipped off to a small city in Gujarat called Navsari, where I was too foreign. Then dropped into an all-girls school in Mumbai, followed by a co-ed high school where my gender-fluid presence was basically the final boss level of social awkwardness. I was taller than most boys—and taller than all expectations.

Throughout my life, I watched my sister shine in every spotlight while I remained the invisible side character with zero plot development. I couldn't speak up, not because I had nothing to say, but because I was terrified of being heard. My words always tripped over themselves, and public speaking felt like walking barefoot over a floor made of Lego.

And then one day, I just . . . stopped. No dramatic revelation. No spiritual retreat. I was simply tired of the performance. I was tired of shrinking myself just to be digestible.

People started calling me crazy. Friends judged. Colleagues gossiped. Lovers ghosted.

Apparently, I was 'too much'. And they were right. I am too much truth, heart, and depth. I'm way too much of someone who's not willing to pretend anymore.

But in that too-muchness, I found peace. Because being 'normal' is a performance I could no longer audition for. I didn't come here to be liked—I came here to live. I came to break patterns, not repeat them.

So, no, I don't want a normal life. I've tried it. It sucked. I'd rather be messy, real, and alive. And if that makes me delusional?

Then, baby, delulu is the solulu!

Assembly Line Rejects

I may be an outcast, but I've always felt a sense of belonging with the ones who shook the world sideways. Remember those renegades?

The ones ridiculed, misunderstood, or politely shoved to the fringes of society while they quietly rewrote the rulebook?

Let's start with sweet, rebellious Galileo. He peeked through a telescope and dared to say: 'Hey guys, I don't think we're the centre of the universe.' The Catholic Church promptly lost its collective halo. They wanted planets orbiting us like fangirls. Galileo was like: 'Nah!' Result? House arrest. Because obviously, the best way to handle groundbreaking science is to ground the scientist.

Then there was Alan Turing, who basically invented the concept of AI before your grandma had a landline. He cracked Nazi codes, birthed computer science, and still had time to be prosecuted for being gay.

And of course, Einstein—the wild-haired wonder who looked like your eccentric uncle with too many cats but casually redefined the entire fabric of space and time while playing the violin. He challenged Newton's laws, slept through fame, and made relativity sound poetic. People thought he was nuts. Turns out, he just saw further.

But science doesn't own the monopoly on misfits. The art world is its own circus of chaos and genius.

Salvador Dalí arrived with melting clocks, dreamscapes on steroids, and a moustache that could probably pick up divine frequencies. Picasso looked at a face and thought: What if we rearranged this like furniture after a messy break-up? People were confused, then captivated, then obsessed.

Vincent van Gogh? Poor man sold barely a painting in his lifetime but became a global icon after cutting off his ear. Today, one sunflower canvas from him could buy you a penthouse in Paris and a backup yacht. And Frida Kahlo? She turned her pain, her politics, and her glorious unibrow into art that still punches patriarchy in the face.

And let's not forget the mystics. The divine lunatics. The holy weirdos.

St Francis of Assisi gave up his rich-boy life to chill with birds and hug people with leprosy. Hildegard of Bingen dropped medieval bangers while casually writing about herbs, healing, and heavenly visions. And Joan of Arc? A literal teenage girlboss who led an army because she heard voices from above. Burned at the stake at nineteen. Canonised later. Classic misfit timeline.

In India, we had Mirabai. A royal turned rebel turned wandering poet, who ditched the palace and sang love songs to Krishna instead. People called her crazy. She called it devotion. And Rumi? That soft-spoken firestorm of a poet who found his divine mirror in a man named Shams and wrote verses that still haunt lovers and seekers alike. Half the internet quotes him without realising he was basically describing ego death and spiritual ecstasy over tea.

And then there was Srinivasa Ramanujan—the Tamil Brahmin who seemed to download complex theorems straight from the Ether. With barely any formal training, he shook the entire Western mathematical community. Scientists are still trying to decode his notes, probably while crying softly into their calculators.

What all these misfits had in common wasn't genius. It was refusal. Refusal to obey the script. They didn't conform, shrink, wait for applause, or a LinkedIn endorsement. They followed the pulse of something deeper, even when the world told them to shut up, sit down, and stay small. They leaned in—louder, weirder, truer.

And yes, many of them were mocked, locked away, cast out, or canonised only once they were dead and no longer inconvenient. Because let's face it: A world obsessed with control doesn't like what it cannot contain. And misfits? They're chaos with a compass.

They take pain and make poetry. They take rejection and reinvent. They don't beg for seats at the table. They build a bonfire outside and make their own circle.

So, if you've ever felt like the black sheep, the odd one out, the one asking questions everyone else was too afraid to voice, take a breath. You're not alone. You're not wrong. You're not broken. You're just not here to repeat what's been done before. You're here to interrupt it.

Because being a misfit isn't a flaw; it's a divine assignment.

Viral Defect

Misfits in the normal world are common. But you'd think that in the rarefied realm of spiritual masters, there'd at least be unity. Agreement. A shared understanding of the whole point of existence. I mean, if there's one club where everyone should be on the same page, it's the club of the 'Awakened Ones', right?

Wrong.

Because just when you thought the spiritual path was a tidy highway of humility, discipline, and enlightenment, along came a Rolls-Royce-driving, truth-spewing wild card who threw glitter bombs and yelled: 'Surprise, bitches!'

That wild card was Bhagwan Shree Rajneesh—later known simply as Osho. And he wasn't here to play by anyone's rules. Especially not the spiritual ones.

Depending on who you ask, Osho was either a spiritual genius or the devil incarnate. Love him or loathe him, the man moved something. He cracked open the sleepy-eyed spiritual scene of the '70s and said: 'Hey, let's add some sex, a disco beat, and brutal honesty to the mix.'

He shook the spiritual world like a snow globe, blending Eastern wisdom with Western rebellion, ancient silence with modern sexuality, sacred stillness with smirking sass. He questioned the system, roasted it, rewrote it, and turned it into an improv monologue about human stupidity.

His real message? Wake the fuck up. Stop playing nice while seething inside. Stop acting like a spiritual robot and pretending you've transcended pain when you haven't even looked your own trauma in the eye. Stop faking serenity just to be liked. Your soul didn't come here to be well-behaved. It came to cause a scene.

But of course, truth-telling doesn't win you brownie points with The System™. Governments, media, and moral police—all clutched their pearls. Cue FBI raids, public meltdowns, and exile drama. Osho went from spiritual celeb to international controversy in record time. And yet, through all the chaos, the heart of his message pulsed strong: Be real.

Osho's madness wasn't madness. It was clarity. He saw through the polished veneers and spiritual cosplay, the lie of conformity dressed up as virtue, the suffocating need to be good, nice, palatable, validated, and approved of. He didn't want spiritual performance. He wanted realness. And realness, it turns out, is terrifying.

Osho didn't care if you liked him. He was here to remind us that even in the spiritual world, the biggest truths sometimes come from the biggest troublemakers. His brand of wisdom didn't come with solace. It came with discomfort, mirrors, and the kind of awkward self-recognition that makes you want to laugh and cry at the same time.

That was his gift. Not certainty, but confusion. Not answers, but a ruthless insistence that you stop lying to yourself.

The Original Blueprint

The thing about misfits—especially the enlightened ones—is that they didn't just challenge the mainstream narrative; they bulldozed it, brick by dogmatic brick.

Every single one of them, in their own way, reached the same conclusion: Our suffering doesn't originate from what's happening out there. It comes from our refusal to see things clearly in here. It's not your boss or annoying in-laws or that flaky friend who only calls when 'Mercury's in Gatorade'. The problem isn't what's happening. It's how we're seeing it—or rather, how we're not.

Reality isn't reality. It's the story we tell ourselves about reality. And those stories are filtered through a brain that's basically running on ancient programming. Think of it like an Instagram filter, but instead of soft lighting, it throws on a fade of childhood trauma, ancestral baggage, fear of rejection, and a little leak of control issues. Suddenly, nothing looks like what it is. Everything's a projection.

The ancient wisdom traditions weren't trying to be deep or poetic when they said the world is an illusion. They were being practical. They saw how we take raw experience, funnel it through our mental noise, and end up living in a hallucination of our own making.

Hinduism called it *Maya*—the grand illusion. Buddhism called it *Samsara*. Christianity brought in the idea of *Original Sin*. Plato gave us the *Cave*. The Sufis spoke of veils separating us from *Haqq*. The Indigenous elders called it the *Great Mystery*.

Different cultures, same message: We're seeing reality through a fogged-up lens.

Because the mind isn't here to show you the truth. It's here to keep you alive. It labels, judges, and memorises past pain and future danger. It's a survival engine, not a clarity machine. So, what do we do? We mistake our thoughts for facts, confuse emotion with intuition, misconstrue the tricks of our ego for the voice of God, project our unresolved mess onto the world—and then get upset when it doesn't behave the way we expected.

But here's the truth: The universe doesn't care about your expectations. It's not trying to hurt you or impress you. It's just doing its thing. It runs on law—cosmic, quiet, unshakeable law.

In India, they call it *Sanatan Dharma*.

Sanatan means 'Eternal' and Dharma means 'Law'. This is neither a religion nor a philosophy. It's the fundamental nature of life itself—or quite simply: The Law of Creation.

Sanatan Dharma is the mathematics and physics of the universe. It's what keeps gravity honest, what holds the galaxies in a spin, and why rivers don't forget where to flow. It's not here to reward or punish. It's simply here to realign you into remembrance.

The ancients didn't need telescopes to see these patterns. They saw them in everything: The spiral of a shell, the rhythm of breath, and the way music vibrates the body into stillness. Because underneath the chaos, there's a pattern so mind-boggling it makes machine learning look like finger painting.

But of course, we thought we could do better. We created laws, broke them, created more. We boxed up the divine, slapped rules on it, and told people how to behave. We tried to replace Dharma with dogma. And somewhere in all that striving, we lost the plot.

One of the most beautiful reminders of Sanatan Dharma lives in three words: *Tat Tvam Asi* (Thou art That). Not 'you should be that', not 'if you meditate hard enough, maybe one day you'll earn that'. Just, you already *are*. The divine isn't out there, hiding behind a Himalayan mountaintop or a bestselling self-help book. It's inside the mess and the mundane. It's inside all of us.

The gods and goddesses with animal heads, extra arms and glowing haloes? They're not fantasy characters. They're metaphors and archetypes representing facets of us—our anger, our love, our stillness, our own chaos. The whole divine spectrum was essentially wrapped in symbolic storytelling.

And science, believe it or not, is finally starting to catch the scent. Quantum physics now tells us matter's mostly empty. That everything's connected. That observation changes what's seen. Turns out, the mystics were never woo-woo; they were just early.

But here's the part most people miss: Knowing isn't enough.

You can study Sanatan Dharma, read the Vedas, memorise the Bhagavad Gita, the Bible, or the Quran. Collect quotes from Rumi and tattoo 'as within so without' on your forearm. But unless you realise it, it's just noise.

Knowing is reading about the taste of mangoes. Realising is biting the mango and letting the juice flood your senses. The truth isn't something you debate with the knowledge you've acquired. It's something you taste.

Manufactured Reality

Stop for a moment and let this sink in: There are over 3,000 planetary systems and around 100-400 billion stars in the Milky Way. That's just our little celestial cul-de-sac. Zoom out and you're staring at two trillion galaxies scattered across space like divine dandruff. And yet here we are—tiny, confused blobs of stardust, doomscrolling and arguing over politics like it's the axis of reality.

Despite Galileo's best attempts to humble us with his discovery that we're *not* the centre of the universe, we still operate like we're the main characters in this galactic drama. Our thoughts? Crucial. Our likes? Sacred. Our barista getting our order wrong? An existential crisis. This species-wide narcissism might just be our biggest blind spot.

This isn't just a 'spiritual' problem—it's biological. Fun fact: Everything we see is actually upside-down before our brain flips it. So even reality comes with a built-in optical illusion. Your nervous system is less National Geographic documentary, more Snapchat filter. It's not showing you the truth. It's showing you the most palatable version you can survive without bursting into tears in the cereal aisle.

So, how do we know what's real?

Let's say you're in a car winding through mountain roads. Your brain feels like it's on a spin cycle. But if you sit cross-legged during that same ride, your body becomes an anchor. The road's still bendy. But you? You're steady. Welcome to the metaphor for life.

Now zoom in from the Milky Way. The Earth spins at about 1,000 miles an hour and orbits the Sun at 67,000 miles an hour. The whole solar system is cartwheeled through the galaxy at over 5,00,000 miles an hour. You're already on a rollercoaster wilder than any amusement park can offer—yet you don't feel it because your senses have adjusted to the motion.

When you sit still in meditation, you're not escaping the ride. You're syncing with it. You're stepping out of the mental fog and remembering that stillness isn't the opposite of movement. It's your anchor in the madness, and that's where the illusion starts to crack.

Maya isn't just about the lack of clarity; it's the normalisation of the spin and getting used to the fog. The confusion becomes familiar, and familiarity starts to feel like truth. Maya convinces us we're separate, isolated planets orbiting our own worlds, spinning in little loops of suffering, believing no one really gets us.

But the truth is far more profound: We're all the same consciousness playing as an avatar.

Meditation isn't about becoming someone new. It's about remembering who's been in there the whole time. It's like Windex for your third eye. The moment you stop fighting the rhythm and start tuning into it, you remember who you are. And this is where it gets delicious!

The third eye isn't a glowing forehead jewel shooting psychic beams at your enemy. It's clarity of perception. It's the moment you stop participating in your life like a Netflix drama and realise you've been the director, producer, scriptwriter, actor, *and* the weepy fan watching reruns.

We've all been little cosmic Pinocchios, tangled in strings of expectation, desire, fear, validation—pretending to be real while slowly forgetting that we already are. We lie to ourselves to keep the plot going. We say we're fine when we're falling apart. We say it's love when it's emotional dependency in a trench coat. We say we're in control when really, we've been hijacked by our own delusions.

But here's the wild part: The puppet master isn't some sinister force pulling your strings. It's your own perception, conditioning, judgement, and biases.

And you can cut the strings.

The yogis knew this long before Western science started poking around with lab coats and EEG machines. Hidden deep in your brain is the pineal gland, aka the original cosmic Wi-Fi router. While modern science credits it with regulating sleep, yogis have always known it as the antenna to higher dimensions. And if it happens to sound suspiciously like Pinocchio—pineal mashed up with *occhio* (Italian for 'eye')—well, maybe Carlo Collodi was onto something.

Either way, you weren't born to stay dizzy, play safe, collect gold stars, or fit neatly into society's little checkbox bingo. You're here to wake up, cut the crap, and remember you were never separate from Source.

Packaging

Much like Pinocchio had to stop lying to become a real boy, we, too, need to drop the lies we tell ourselves if we want to meet life as it truly is. Because let's face it—if Newton could discover gravity from a rogue apple, imagine what we could unlock if we just sat under a tree long enough.

Enter: Yoga.

No, not goat yoga, hot yoga, beer yoga, or the kind that comes bundled with a juice cleanse and a sound bath. I'm talking about the original technology of self-realisation, which breaks your illusions, not your hamstrings.

Yoga literally means 'union'. It's a system designed to crack through illusion, align your body, mind, and energy, bringing you back into harmony with the source of creation. It doesn't want you to escape the human experience. It wants you to experience it fully.

In yogic science, the human experience is said to unfold through *Pancha Koshas*, or the five sheaths or layers of consciousness that shape how we perceive reality. Each layer is a level of consciousness, a different way of experiencing reality. Think of them like layers of a cosmic cake—except instead of icing and sponge, you get perception and transcendence.

1D: Annamaya Kosha (The Food Body)

This is your physical body—the one that bloats after pizza and has opinions about mirror lighting. Made from food, sustained by food, and eventually composted back into food. This is the part of you that gets sunburnt, stubbed, judged, moisturised, and sometimes worshipped. But don't get too attached, because it's just the biodegradable packaging.

2D: Manomaya Kosha (The Mental Body)

Welcome to your internal group chat. This is where your thoughts, emotions, dreams, flashbacks, imaginary arguments, and that one awkward thing you said in 2012 all hang out. Most of us live here full-time, trapped in a loop of overthinking, comparing, catastrophising, and calling it productivity.

3D: Pranamaya Kosha (The Energy Body)

Now we're talking electricity. This is the power grid of your system that animates everything. Every breath, blink, goosebump, orgasm, that's Pranamaya in action. It flows through 72,000 *Nadis* (energy channels) and gathers at 112 *Chakras* (junction points). And just like the wind powers a wind turbine, our breath powers *Prana* (the life force). Pranayama, or the art of breathwork, is designed to tune the frequency of your life force. This is why a few simple breathing exercises can shift your vibe from 'perpetually overwhelmed' to 'cool as a cucumber'.

4D: Vigyanamaya Kosha (The Knowledge Body)

This is the kosha that sees through the nonsense and intuitively senses things. In 4D, you start recognising patterns and realise that the toxic ex wasn't a punishment but a plot device. That job loss wasn't chaos but a course correction. You don't just react, you witness. You stop buying into your identity like it's a forever contract and begin seeing yourself as consciousness in costume.

5D: Anandamaya Kosha (The Bliss Body)

This is the final sheath that experiences itself as one with everything in the universe. It is the deep, silent joy that isn't disturbed by anything external. It's what remains when the dust settles, the roles drop, and you're no longer trying to prove anything. This is what you experience when all the separateness dissolves into oneness.

These koshas aren't steps on a spiritual staircase. They're happening all at once, layered like browser tabs in your consciousness. You're not here to 'transcend' them but rather become aware of them.

For this purpose, yoga is the user manual. It doesn't promise instant bliss or a dramatic soul glow-up, but it does give you tools to live from alignment, instead of autopilot. It allows you to experience union not as a theory, but a living reality.

Quality Control

People talk about protecting energy and balancing chakras as if it is a weekend project, but honestly, how can you balance something you don't even feel?

You see, your body isn't just biology; it's a complex architecture of energy channels, circuits, junctions, and command centres. Practices like yoga, meditation, and pranayama align and sensitise you to these subtler dimensions of life.

According to yogic science, there are seven major chakras, each one tied to a layer of human experience. Just as a house has rooms that gather dust, so, too, do these centres carry your unresolved grief, guilt, desires, and delusions. Each of these chakras has both light and shadow.

Interestingly, the shadows of these chakras align with the 'Seven Deadly Sins' in Christianity. Not in a religious, guilt-trip kind of way, but as poetic clues. Each 'sin' isn't a moral failure but rather a feedback loop saying, 'Hey, something's off. Come back.'

Let's walk through the house.

1. The Basement: Root Chakra (*Muladhara*)
Function: Foundation, safety, survival
Deadly Sin: Gluttony

This is the floor you walk on. Muladhara is the part of you that wants to feel safe, fed, and not constantly in fight-or-flight. When this room is sturdy, you move through life with grounded ease, trusting that you're safe and secure. But when fear cracks the foundation, Gluttony seeps in. The hunger and compulsive grab for anything that looks like security: Attention, validation, people who feel like home but burn like hell. You start collecting anchors instead of building roots, and the house shakes.

2. The Bathroom: Sacral Chakra (*Svadhisthana*)
Function: Emotion, pleasure, intimacy
Deadly Sin: Lust

This is where things flow—be it water or emotions. This is the part of the house where you release, cleanse, and occasionally sob in the shower for reasons unknown. When Svadhisthana is in balance, you honour your emotions, enjoy your body, and don't treat pleasure like a crime. But when this room gets flooded or locked up, lust leaks in. You chase sensation without satisfaction—constantly trying to *feel* something but avoiding real depth.

3. The Kitchen: Solar Plexus (*Manipura*)
Function: Power, identity, will
Deadly Sin: Greed

This is the heart of the house. The fire. The 'I do' and 'I am'. This is where your confidence cooks and where your boundaries get baked. When Manipura is strong, you move with self-respect and you own your choices and your time. But leave this fire rage unchecked, and greed comes in hot. You start measuring your worth in output. Ambition and productivity become your drug. You hoard time, power, attention and status, thinking more will finally make you feel *worthy*. But the fire doesn't feed you. It devours you.

4. The Living Room: Heart Chakra (*Anahata*)
Function: Love, connection, forgiveness
Deadly Sin: Envy

This is the heart of the home where people gather and where feelings are shared. When the Anahata is open, the room breathes with creativity. There's warmth, belonging and love without needing to be owned. But when this room closes, Envy moves in like an unwanted guest. You start eyeing other people's joy as if it's a limited resource. You compare relationships, bodies, success and timelines. You forget that love isn't a rationed commodity but a frequency. One you can always tune into if you'd just stop flipping the channel.

5. The Study: Throat Chakra (*Vishuddhi*)
Function: Expression, truth, communication
Deadly Sin: Wrath

This is your internal broadcast station with a desk, mic, and journal. When the Vishuddhi is open, you lead with confidence and power. You don't shrink or scream but speak with clarity and courage. However, when you silence this room for too long, Wrath finds the cracks. First in sarcasm, then in passive aggression, and finally in full-blown volcanic eruptions over your WhatsApp privacy lock. Because when truth is exiled, it festers and, believe me, it will find a way out, one way or another.

6. The Attic: Third Eye (*Ajna*)
Function: Insight, intuition, perception
Deadly Sin: Sloth

This is the tower with the window that overlooks it all. When Ajna is clear, you see patterns, connect dots others miss, and act not from impulse but from vision. You witness instead of reacting. But the shadow here is a tricky one. Sloth. Not couch-potato laziness, but the kind of avoidance that wears a spiritual hoodie and calls itself 'non-attachment'. You know what needs to change, but you refuse to change because doing the real work is just too damn hard.

7. The Roof: Crown Chakra (*Sahasrara*)
Function: Unity, consciousness, transcendence
Deadly Sin: Pride

This is the rooftop where the house ends and the sky begins. When the Sahasrara is open, there's no 'me' and 'them'. There's just consciousness playing different characters, remembering itself through every interaction. But pride can sneak in here disguised as enlightenment. You start believing you've 'arrived'. That others don't get it like you do, and you're above the mess. You build a spiritual identity with better branding and forget that wisdom doesn't shout from the rooftop; it simply stands tall.

Each chakra is a doorway, and each sin is just a sign you forgot where the door was. The higher you rise, the more you land.

But here's the catch: Having the house is one thing, living in it consciously is another. Most of us move through our inner architecture like distracted tenants; leaving lights on, locking doors we need open, ignoring leaks until the ceiling caves in. If you really want to evolve, you can't just own the house. You have to watch it closely because every creak and crack is actually feedback.

Surveillance Room

Now, if you're truly serious about evolving, you need to learn the art of paying attention. And I don't mean the performative head-tilt you give in meetings while mentally drafting your grocery list. I mean the kind of attention that rewires perception, strips away the default lens, and forces you to see life as it is: complex, layered, and unmistakably tailored for your awakening.

Because reality, as chaotic as it seems, is not random. It's a meticulously crafted, full-spectrum, interactive feedback loop designed to reflect your consciousness to you in high definition. The people, patterns, drama, algorithms, headlines, heartbreaks—they're all part of a vast hall of mirrors, each one offering a glimpse of something you've projected, inherited, denied, or forgotten.

The universe is staging a full-blown interactive theatre piece called 'This Is You'.

Ever heard a song that felt like it cracked open your ribcage? Or watched a film that somehow knew your entire relationship history? It's because the universe doesn't communicate in bullet points. It speaks in resonance. And anything that moves you deeply, disturbingly, or inexplicably is doing so because it carries a frequency you already hold.

Take *Harry Potter*, for instance. It's not just about a boy battling a noseless creep with a snake fetish. It's about light and shadow, love over fear, and the deeply magical architecture of existence. Hogwarts isn't a school; it's an energetic realm and a metaphor for the invisible dimensions that live side by side with the boring Muggle matrix most of us call reality.

The same with the movie *Interstellar*. People thought it was a film about space and science, but it was actually a cosmic love letter. Time isn't linear. Gravity gets weird. And love? It might just be the Wi-Fi of the universe. You already knew all this—you just needed Matthew McConaughey whispering it from a tesseract to remind you.

Even shows like *Game of Thrones*, *Squid Game*, or *Black Mirror*, soaked in blood and betrayal, are more than binge-worthy chaos. They're dark mirrors reflecting the collective human shadow: Power games, greed, inequality, moral compromise. These stories slap us across the face and say, 'Look at what you've built. Look at what you've normalised.'

What makes these stories grip the globe isn't their production value but their honesty. They reflect a truth we often deny: That we are capable of beauty, betrayal, creation, cruelty, transcendence, and collapse—all in the span of a single human lifetime.

And the mirrors don't stop at fiction. Technology has joined the theatre. The internet, in all its invisible reach, is simply a digital mimicry of the energetic grid that underlies reality. We didn't invent connectivity—we just copied it, gave it a brand name, and slapped on a subscription fee.

The cloud is our clumsy version of the Akashic Records. Instant messaging is diet telepathy. Video calls are basically teleportation. Google is our attempt at tapping into collective consciousness without actually meditating. Everything we've built online is a digital photocopy of our innate abilities—just with a little more buffering.

Artificial Intelligence (AI), too, is being marketed as the next leap in human innovation when, in truth, it's merely the latest mirror. It sees, learns, adapts, and creates patterns from input. Sound familiar? That's *Consciousness 101.* We've been doing that since birth: Taking in stimuli, shaping identity, running scripts inherited from generations past.

Everything we've ever built externally is a reflection of something we already sensed internally. Planes echoed birds. Solar panels echoed leaves. The web echoed intuition. And the more we attempt to refine these tools, the more we unwittingly confront the raw, uncomfortable truth: Our technology is not separate from us; it is us, amplified.

But amplification works both ways. The internet can connect or divide. AI can enlighten or exploit. These tools reveal not their own nature, but ours. The chaos isn't in the machine—it's in the consciousness that programmed it. They're reflections of us. So, if we're afraid that AI might turn against us and destroy the world one day, it's only because we're running on toxic patterns we've refused to clean up.

That's why consciousness matters. If we don't develop our consciousness—our capacity to witness, to choose, to evolve—we'll get lost in the very mirrors we made. Surrounded by tech that reflects us better than we've ever reflected on ourselves. This isn't a warning; it's an invitation to wake up, look around, and see the world as one giant reflection of what's going on within.

The people who annoy you? They're teachers.
The lovers who leave you? They're mirrors.
The news that makes you spiral? They're clues.
There is no 'out there'.
There is only 'in here'.

And the moment you stop blaming the mirror for what it reflects, you reclaim your power to shift what gets projected.

SOLULU 1
Face Your Triggers

Pain is essentially your soul waving a giant neon sign that says, 'Hey, something's off!' Cut your finger, and the blood screams, 'Dress this wound.' Emotional pain? Same thing. But instead of listening, most of us treat our feelings like spam e-mail: We ignore, delete, or silently pray they vanish on their own.

Spoiler alert: They don't. They simply go underground, start a group chat, and invite more unresolved feelings to the party.

The only way out? Face the mess and become a detective of your own dysfunction.

First things first: Drop the act. You're not supposed to be perfect. Nobody is. Everyone is a little unhinged; some of us just accessorise it better. Accepting that deranged is the default setting is wildly liberating. It means you can stop performing sanity and start getting real.

But let's be clear: Acceptance isn't code for lashing out irresponsibly. It doesn't mean, 'Oh well, I guess, I'll just be my toxic self.' Nah! It means starting where you are with brutal honesty, a touch of grace, and the decision not to spiritually ghost yourself any longer.

Triggers are simply unhealed wounds, and every time someone or something pokes that tender spot, it's not *their* fault. It's your body saying, 'Sweetie, we still haven't dealt with this.' The mature thing? Stop pointing fingers like a conspiracy theorist with a red string board and start pointing the flashlight inward. Even when it really feels like it's someone else's fault, it's not about them. It's about you.

Your triggers are your responsibility. The world does not owe you a 'trigger warning'. Life isn't here to make you comfortable. If something hurts, let it hurt. Feel it fully. Mourn it dramatically. Cry like the lead in a tragic indie film. Because when you stop avoiding and start feeling, something magical happens: The drama begins to dissolve. You get curious. You ask, 'Wait . . . am I actually dying, or did my ego just get a paper cut?'

That's when pain alchemises into wisdom and self-pity morphs into self-awareness. Slowly, the need to blame begins to fade. And every time you unhook from a delusion about yourself, others, or the world, the trigger loses its power. The gun's still there, yes. But it's empty. And eventually, you're not flinching anymore.

The universe isn't punishing you; it's just following a pattern. Every villain, heartbreak, and awkward encounter is designed to reveal the magnificent design of creation. You can only perceive it if you pay keen attention and stop taking everything personally.

It turns out there are no glitches in the matrix. Only our misperception that there's one.

Yes, hurt people hurt people. But healed people? They break the cycle.

Welcome to the work. It's messy, holy, and hilarious!

Delulu 2

THE INTELLECTUAL IS INTELLIGENT

'There is so much to read.
There are so many concepts.
There are so many teachings.
You will become a very intelligent idiot.'

– Robert Adams

ORIENTATION DAY

In today's chaotic carnival of existence, education is treated like the holy grail. From the moment we wobble into a classroom clutching oversized backpacks and oversized expectations, we're told the road to success is paved with perfect report cards and laminated degrees.

Grades become gospel, degrees become destiny, and universities turn into factories where futures are manufactured—one PowerPoint at a time. And, God forbid, you colour outside the lines—that's a one-way ticket to 'concerned parent' WhatsApp groups and awkward career counselling sessions dripping with shame.

Education is sold to us like insurance. Want stability? Get a degree. Want respect? Add some acronyms after your name. Want to matter? Frame that diploma and stare at it daily. But here's a question: What if this sacred compass to success isn't pointing north at all? What if we've just been circling a fancy fountain of mediocrity?

Because let's be honest: Most of what we call 'education' is high-functioning parroting. It's not learning—it's performance. Memorise, regurgitate, compete, compare, repeat. We spend two decades solving problems we'll never face, with tools we don't understand, for approval we don't even believe in.

We can list thirty rivers, yet not know how to connect with our own breath. We're taught how to pass tests but not how to pass through life without becoming a burnt-out husk with a LinkedIn profile and no will to live.

What if education isn't meant to fill you up but empty you out? What if the real point is to strip away noise, false identities and hand-me-down beliefs—to make space for something more alive? What if learning's true purpose is to help you tune in to the intelligence already buzzing in your bones?

Because once upon a time, it was.

Long before boardrooms and classroom bells, knowledge wasn't about information; it was about transformation. Around 3,000 BCE, education systems guided human evolution, not just employment. Education was holistic, and enlightenment—not employability—was the endgame. But where did this wisdom first sprout?

Legend says that 15,000 years ago, in the frosty Himalayas, a mysterious man appeared. No name tag, no business card—just vibes. Wrapped in silence, he sat beneath the open sky, spine straighter than your straightest mate.

Okay, I know what you could be thinking: 'Excuse me, did you just say 15,000 years ago?' Yes, I did. And no, I don't have carbon-dated receipts or a mystical Fitbit from the Pleistocene. If you're after evidence, I'm fresh out of time machines and unwilling to battle Google for archaeological clout.

What I do have is a potent cocktail of intuition, ancient whispers, hard-earned insights and a dash of 'just go with it.' So, if you're willing to suspend disbelief—and maybe a few degrees—you might enjoy the ride.

No pressure to believe me. In fact, I'd prefer you didn't. Because what follows isn't necessarily history; it's the story of how learning was never meant to chain us to a desk, but to unshackle us from illusion.

Class is officially in session!

CLASS TEACHER

Fifteen thousand years ago, a crowd gathered around this mysterious figure, buzzing with expectation. Maybe he'd levitate or drop a sermon with subtitles. Instead, this half-ash, half-enigma just danced—wild, ecstatic.

And when they thought he'd speak in tongues, he dropped into silence. Days turned to weeks, months, and years without food or water. Not even a suspicious glance at the nearest bush for a loo break. He just sat there, like a loading screen stuck at 99 per cent.

Seven souls, either unusually curious or alarmingly unemployed, decided he clearly knew something. They sat at his feet, not for blessings or selfies, but begging him to reveal the secret behind his cosmic high.

But enlightenment wasn't served on a brass platter. This wasn't a weekend workshop. He tested them, pushed them to the edge, stripped away everything they thought they knew. Months blurred into years of penance, through which they expanded and evolved.

Finally, when they were ready, he led them to the crystalline shores of Kanti Sarovar. Under the full moon—nature's original screensaver—they embarked on a crash course in life's deepest mysteries. That full moon night, now marked as Guru Purnima, transformed him from Adiyogi (first yogi) to Guru.

He shared 112 techniques for human mastery, mirroring the 112 chakras in the human system. Not just stretches or breathwork, but a complete operating manual for evolution. Yoga, literally meaning 'union', became the key to dissolving the illusion of separation and perceiving reality with crystal clarity.

His seven disciples, the *Saptrishis*, were the first to 'drop out of the matrix'. They carried his teachings across continents, cultures and time—blueprints for spiritual distribution long before missionaries were a thing.

One, Agastya Muni, travelled across India as the original cultural influencer. Temple layouts, sitting cross-legged, the greeting of *Namaste*, eating with our hands—it was all intentional design. Yoga became a way of life, the root of Sanatan Dharma, and the seed behind the Vedas, Upanishads, Puranas, and all that bloomed from mystical India.

At the heart of it all stood Shiva. *Shi-va* literally means 'that which is not', the vast, boundless space from which everything originates and to which it returns. They called Adiyogi 'Shiva' because through his methods they glimpsed the source of creation—a no-thing.

This no-thingness, this emptiness, isn't absence but infinite potential. From this stillness, creation begins its dance: Birth, death, destruction, renewal—all spinning in divine rhythm. The cosmic Nataraja is Shiva's metaphor for the universe's heartbeat.

And this isn't just mythology—it's physics. At CERN (Conseil Européen pour la Recherche Nucléaire), the global HQ for people who split atoms before lunch, a statue of Nataraja stands with a plaque quoting physicist Fritjof Capra from his book *The Tao of Physics*:

> Hundreds of years ago, Indian artists created visual images of dancing Shivas in a beautiful series of bronzes. In our

> time, physicists have used the most advanced technology to portray the patterns of the cosmic dance. The metaphor of the cosmic dance thus unifies ancient mythology, religious art and modern physics.

In *The Tao of Physics*, Capra drew striking parallels between Shiva's dance and subatomic motion—matter as energy, in constant flux. Ancient sages and modern scientists describe the same thing, just in different accents.

Even nuclear reactors—those vast vessels harnessing raw energy—are modelled after the Shiva Linga. Not because someone felt spiritual, but because the ellipsoidal form is known to hold and distribute energy most efficiently.

The ancients weren't dreamers; they were engineers of the unseen, tuning into frequencies we're only now measuring. Their rituals weren't random, their structures weren't decorative—they were blueprints aligning human consciousness with the cosmos.

The first guru wasn't building a religion. He simply handed humanity a mirror, reminding us that the wisdom we seek has always lived inside. All we need is to sit still long enough to hear it.

Sacred Curriculum

After Adiyogi and his seven spiritual storm-chasers sketched the blueprint for inner transformation, the architecture echoed beyond the Himalayas. It rippled across millennia and continents, embedding itself into the bones of early civilisations, laying the foundations of sacred systems for seeking.

In Egypt around 3,000 BCE, temples weren't built only to immortalise kings in eyeliner or stack tombs with luxury-grade afterlife luggage. The *Per Ankh*, or House of Life, was a spiritual laboratory—half university, half portal—where priest-scholars mapped constellations, decoded sacred geometry, and recorded what was received in trance. Knowledge was sacred. Education was initiation.

By 1,500 BCE, humanity's thirst for meaning had gone viral. The raw transmissions of seers and sages crystallised into doctrine, ritual, and scripture. Enter: Religion, version 1.0. Fewer cave echoes, more structure. Less ecstasy, more curriculum.

In India, two royal dropouts made headlines. Buddha left behind a palace and a haircare routine to sit under a tree and solve the riddle of suffering. His answer was simple: Life hurts, desire traps, and awareness liberates.

Mahavira, by contrast, stripped life to its moral atoms. No violence. No lies. No frills. Just pure, ascetic clarity. A moral minimalism so stark it made Marie Kondo look like a hoarder.

Meanwhile in Persia, Zoroaster staged the great cosmic drama: Light versus dark, good versus evil. His vision didn't demand ritual compliance but action with integrity. Choose truth, live it. Easy to say, harder to swipe right on.

In ancient China, Laozi dropped the *Tao Te Ching* like a philosophical mixtape. Less grind, more glide. Harmony over hustle. He invented 'go with the flow' centuries before it became a bumper sticker.

Over in Greece, Plato and Aristotle launched the first season of 'Philosophical Idol'. Their schools, the *Academy* and the *Lyceum*, were idea factories turning out timeless thought on ethics, logic, and metaphysics. By now, education was structured and soul-deep.

Meanwhile, India was pulling off a full-blown educational renaissance. Between 1,500 and 500 BCE, the Vedic and later Buddhist traditions built an educational system unlike anything the world had seen. Sanskrit and Pali weren't just languages; they were frequency codes. Their phonetics were tuned to body, breath, brain, and consciousness.

The curriculum didn't aim only to inform. It was built to transform. The Vedas sang of cosmic order. The Upanishads whispered of the one self behind all selves. The Dharmasutras mapped ethics with surgical precision. Study spanned architecture, astronomy, logic, linguistics, medicine, music, and metaphysics—all designed to produce not specialists but sovereigns: Humans capable of holding complexity without being torn apart.

The Vedangas were its limbs: *Shiksha* (phonetics) to pronounce truth, *Vyakarana* (grammar) to structure it, *Chandas* (metre) to feel it, *Nirukta* (etymology) to trace it, *Kalpa* (ritual) to embody it, and *Jyotishya* (astronomy) to align it with cosmic order.

There were electives, too: *Gandharva Veda* (Music), vibrational medicine to reshape inner chemistry and *Ayurveda* (Medicine), which saw disease as disharmony and sought balance, not relief.

Students didn't get gold stars for attendance. They walked barefoot into forests, lived in *gurukuls*, washed their teacher's feet, starved their ego, and sharpened their perception. Graduation didn't mean a degree but the dissolving of self. This sacred fire lit Takshashila and Nalanda, universities where peasants and princes learnt side by side.

Then came a man who walked barefoot, spoke in parables, and said the Kingdom of God wasn't up there but within. Jesus Christ didn't institutionalise spirituality. He humanised it. His message was simple: Love, forgive, and see God in the poor, the broken, and the forgotten. His classroom was wherever someone was ready to listen.

From there, the torch moved on. Monks in Europe guarded sacred texts with candlelight and ink. In the Islamic world, madrasas became epicentres of knowledge, blending Quranic wisdom with algebra and astronomy. The Jewish Beit Midrash kept questioning alive as devotion.

And then came the whirr.

The 18th century brought the Industrial Revolution and rearranged the whole show.

Suddenly, we went from 'Who am I?' to 'Will this be on the exam?'

Mass Indoctrination

In the early 19th century, a group of very serious men in Prussia looked at children and thought, 'You know what would make them thrive? Factory settings.' Thus was born the blueprint we still haven't escaped—valuing conformity over curiosity, efficiency over exploration, obedience over originality.

The open wonder of gurukuls was shown the door. Mechanisation and monotony marched in with pressed collars and clipboards.

As industrialisation tore through society like a hyper-caffeinated hurricane, education became less about awakening and more about assembling. The system wasn't built to elevate consciousness. It was built to keep children seated, sorted, and silent. Classrooms became conveyor belts where young minds were processed, packaged, and stamped.

Fast forward a couple of centuries, and the ghost of that model still lingers—haunting boards, hijacking syllabi, politely crushing the spirit of children who only want to know why clouds look like dinosaurs. Instead, they're forced to memorise when Vasco da Gama set sail and why mitochondria is the powerhouse of the cell.

We've produced generations of obedient citizens—predictable workers who follow orders, pay taxes, and question authority only when it trends on Twitter. Minds cluttered with facts they'll never use. Hearts closed to wonder. Souls, waiting for permission to be curious.

As I said at the start of this book, I wasn't exactly student-of-the-month. I spent most of school avoiding maths and waiting for recess or P. E. Only English and Geography ever landed—words and worlds. English gave me metaphors for the chaos inside. Geography fed my need to understand the chaos outside. The rest was a blurry slideshow of facts I was meant to care about but didn't.

I never let school brainwash me. I didn't buy into the gold-star economy. I wasn't seduced by grades or terrified by red pens. I cared more about people than performance. I gravitated towards teachers with soul—those rare few whose eyes carried the weight of real life. They were the true curriculum.

And sometimes, let's be honest, I crushed hard on my teachers. I felt a soul connect. I'd study them like I would an indie musician or an unrequited love. Their walk, their style, their voice, their life outside school, the way they smiled when a point lit the room. I lingered after class just to stay in their orbit.

It wasn't romantic as much as it was a hunger to be seen—to feel chosen by someone wise and extraordinary. When you're a sensitive child adrift in the void of modern schooling, a teacher who 'gets you' is a lighthouse in the fog.

Looking back, I see those crushes for what they were: Longing in disguise. Longing for mentorship, resonance, and affirmation that I wasn't invisible. Maybe that's what made school tolerable. Fleeting moments of connection that reminded me I was more than just another name on a roll call.

The rest of school felt like a long, slow trudge through a maze designed by someone who disliked children. We raised hands, lowered voices, sat still even when everything inside begged to move. And though I resisted, I wasn't immune. I still felt the gnawing ache of unworthiness.

Because school isn't just education; it's a hierarchy. A Student Council. A Head Prefect. A Star Pupil. Names engraved on plaques as if ancient gods of achievement. Even if I didn't chase top grades, I felt the sting of being unseen. I wasn't the rebel, the genius, or the teacher's pet. I was just . . . a child. And apparently, that wasn't enough.

School never rewarded depth. It rewarded performance. And when your essence is absent from roll calls and honour boards, you start to wonder if you matter. You internalise the idea that visibility must be earned—that unless you're exceptional, you're forgettable.

No wonder burnout now hits before the first pay cheque.

The Prussian model didn't just fail us—it programmed us to fail ourselves. So, here we are, perfectionism in one hand, impostor syndrome in the other, and a lifetime supply of anxiety asking, 'Am I good enough yet?'

Mental Detention

School was easier to dodge than college. Suddenly, I was surrounded by people who casually quoted Shakespeare while brushing their teeth. People who'd read *War and Peace* for fun. I, meanwhile, thought 'Dostoevsky' was a brand of vodka. So, I did what any self-respecting imposter would do: I faked it.

I launched 'Operation Pretend to Be Smart'. I clutched a thesaurus like it was my emotional support animal. I threw big words into every sentence as if I were being paid per syllable. My essays dripped with phrases like 'post-colonial somatic fragmentation' and 'hegemonic dissonance', as if I were trying to out-intellectual Foucault. On the outside, I looked like I had it all figured out. Inside? I was a human panic room with zero ventilation.

The symptoms worsened further in university. This wasn't just academic cosplay anymore; this was supposed to be the beginning of my 'career'. But even then, I couldn't focus in class. I'd zone out mid-lecture, thinking about everything from the existence of parallel universes to whether my professor was having an affair with the librarian.

By the time education was done with me, I had a PhD in Pretentiousness and a minor in Judging People. Because here's the thing they don't teach you in lecture halls: Knowledge isn't wisdom, and buying gym clothes doesn't make you fit.

The intellect is seductive. It flatters you into thinking you're growing when, really, you're just getting better at Googling. It builds castles in your mind and then locks you inside without a key. It gives you a false sense of superiority, disguising fear and insecurity as 'critical thinking'.

After my graduation in 2016, armed with a shiny international degree and a bleeding heart, I marched into the social sector. I became the youngest board member at a feminist non-profit, and I thought I was doing 'real work'. But in reality, I was simply drowning in PowerPoint presentations and internalised rage.

I judged people who worked in offices. I judged heteronormative people. People who said 'holistic' but meant 'expensive' were instantly suspect. Honestly, I judged everyone—because deep down, I still hadn't looked in the mirror.

Eventually, burnout came for me like a debt collector, and I realised something both obvious and horrifying: My activism wasn't rooted in compassion. It was fuelled by unprocessed pain. As it turns out, when your activism comes from a wound, it doesn't heal. It just spreads the wound around in fancier packaging.

That's when the penny dropped. My righteousness wasn't about truth. It was a survival strategy—a glorified escape hatch from vulnerability. I wore my opinions like armour, but all they really did was keep love out and shame in.

Here we must pause for a very important public service announcement: There is a colossal difference between intellect and intelligence.

Intellect is flashy. It's the sharp machete of the mind, quick to slice and eager to prove. It loves being right. It thrives in debates, dominates in discussions, and will quote obscure thinkers in bed if given half a chance. But intelligence is quieter and more grounded. It's the gardener of awareness. It knows when to prune and when to wait. It doesn't need to win. It only wants to understand.

Intellect builds arguments. Intelligence builds bridges.

Intellect obsesses over appearances. Intelligence listens for patterns in silence.

Intellect gets you awards. Intelligence gets you peace.

The inconvenient truth no one wants to write in bold font on a college prospectus: Intelligence isn't additive. It's subtractive. You don't become wise by knowing more; you become wise by carrying less. Less ego. Less certainty. Less need to be seen.

Eventually, I had to burn the curriculum of self-importance, put down the need to be the smartest person in the room, and start becoming the most honest.

At first, unlearning felt like failure. As though all the books I'd underlined and all the essays I'd written had amounted to nothing. But slowly, something softer emerged: The kind of intelligence that didn't need to announce itself. That didn't rely on aesthetics, academic lingo, or social justice theatre to feel valuable. An intelligence that could sit with contradiction and still choose compassion.

When I started walking barefoot into the messy terrain of my own heart, that was the turning point. I stopped performing knowledge and started embodying wisdom when I was able to be honest with myself and ask the harder questions: 'Where am I avoiding my own healing?' and 'What would my activism look like if it were rooted in love instead of rage?'

Theory of Knowledge

For most of human history, we've asked, 'How can we know, and how can we be sure?' A noble pursuit, no doubt. But after a few thousand years of arguing over semantics, we've always ended up with more data than direction.

Western logic, bless its obsessive heart, spent centuries trying to dissect the nature of reality using tools built from the very thing it was dissecting: The mind. It's like trying to taste your own tongue or Photoshop your own eyeballs. Impressive effort but fundamentally flawed.

What began as a noble quest for truth often turned into an academic ouroboros: Rational thought chasing its own tail, publishing papers about the tail, and hosting TED Talks on the nuances of tail-chasing.

The yogic sciences, however, took a different route. Where modern systems dissected the universe to know more, Yoga turned inwards and asked, 'What if you stopped trying to figure it all out and just . . . became it?' It didn't discard the intellect; it simply refused to let it drive the whole cart.

Yoga suggested that understanding reality wasn't a matter of sharpening the mind but of expanding the self. And to do that, it mapped four distinct faculties through which we access knowledge: Body, mind, emotion, and energy.

Gyana Yoga (Path of Knowledge—Mind)

This is the path for the overthinkers, the philosophers, the inner narrators who can't stop spiralling into questions like, 'What is the point of all this?' But Gyana yoga doesn't hand you answers on a plate. It hands you a mirror and urges you to look deeper. It's a method of self-inquiry designed to slice through the noise of identity, memory, ideology, and illusion until all that's left is direct knowing. You don't arrive at truth through logic; you arrive by watching logic collapse under the weight of its own limitations.

Karma Yoga (Path of Action—Body)

If Gyana is about questioning reality, Karma is about showing up in it. This is about action as spiritual practice. Not performance, people-pleasing, or checklist-driven self-worth, but the quiet art of doing what's required in the world without clinging to the outcome or obsessing over credit. Whether you're washing dishes or leading a revolution, Karma yoga asks: Can you act without being hijacked by identity? Can you serve without turning it into a brand? With Karma, every action becomes an opportunity to dissolve the ego. And when you stop performing your goodness, you become good without trying.

Kriya Yoga (Path of Kriya—Energy)

This is the path for those who learn through doing. Not externally like Karma, but internally—with breath, sensation, vibration, and inner alchemy. Kriya works on the subtle body: The circuits of prana, or life force, that animate everything from your heartbeat to your intuition. It uses techniques such as breathwork, sound, mudras, and movement to rewire how energy flows through you. If your mind is the software and your body is the hardware, Kriya is the electricity that makes it all run. And when practised correctly, it bypasses words and goes straight into transformation without the need to intellectualise it to death.

Bhakti Yoga (Path of Devotion—Emotion)

If Gyana untangles the mind, Karma refines your action, and Kriya rewires your energy, then Bhakti walks straight into the heart and asks, 'What are you willing to surrender?' At its core, Bhakti is about *love*. Not belief in a concept, but intimacy with someone or something else that you can put above your own self. For some, it's a god; for some, a guru; for some a lover or child. All of it counts—because Bhakti is about finding a depth of love that requires you to let go of control.

Of all these, Bhakti is the fastest route to self-realisation. But it is also the most difficult, because you can't game this path. There's no strategy, no reward points, no higher score for good behaviour. Only the capacity to love for love's sake. And that kind of vulnerability? Terrifying . . . but also transformational.

Because this path teaches you something the others can't: That real love is not a feeling, it's a furnace. It melts your defences, fries your superiority complex, and strips your ego. Real devotion will have you lying on your bathroom floor at 3:17 a.m., mascara smudged, and heart cracked wide open, whispering into the void, 'Even now, I trust you.'

Bhakti doesn't ask for your resumé. It asks whether you can trust while trembling, whether you can love without needing a guarantee, and whether you're willing to be changed by something you can't fully explain.

'Love is the fulfilling of the law,' wrote Saint Paul.

Translation?

If Dharma is the eternal law, then 'love' is the password that logs you into the source.

CLASS TOPPER

If you're still thinking devotion is just for sentimental aunties with flower baskets and leaky tear ducts, think again. Devotion is not soft. It is savage. It doesn't gently nudge your ego towards enlightenment; it unhinges its jaw and swallows it whole.

And no one understood this better than Mirabai, a 16th-century Rajput princess turned mystic, who turned her back on palaces, pearls, and political alliances to chase Krishna.

As a child, she once saw a statue of Krishna and asked her mother, 'Who is my husband?' Her mother, caught off guard (and probably halfway through a samosa), pointed at the idol and said, 'He is.' Most children would have forgotten that by lunchtime, but Mira took it to heart and made it her life's mission.

That one offhand comment lit the fuse. While the other queens obsessed over court gossip and sari drapes, Mira was locking herself in her chambers, writing love poetry to a god who never wrote back. She wept in longing, danced in love, and sang as though the whole cosmos was listening. And maybe it was.

Of course, the palace was not impressed. Her royal in-laws considered her disgraceful. A princess in love with a statue? They tried to shame her, isolate her, and eventually poison her. But Mirabai didn't flinch. According to legend, she drank the poison and lived because Bhakti makes you immune to the venom of this world.

Eventually, she left the palace behind. No mic-drop moment, no farewell letter, just her anklets jingling as she wandered from temple to temple, singing songs for her beloved.

One of her verses goes like this:

Mere to Giridhar Gopal, dūsro na koi.
Main to unke rang rachi rahi,
aur rang na dooja koi.

[I am dyed in the colour of my beloved,
I have become one with him.
Call me by any name, it makes no difference.]

She didn't read scriptures to understand love. She *became* love so completely that the scriptures started reading her.

Legend says that Mirabai's devotion reached such heights that one day, in Dwarka, she walked into the sanctum of Krishna's temple and simply vanished, leaving behind only her anklets. Gone. Merged. Dissolved. *Poof!*

This is yogic physics. In the ancient traditions of India, there are stories of saints and yogis who, having mastered their prana, could dematerialise their bodies at will and leave behind nothing but a puddle of water. This isn't death. It's conscious dissolution—a return to the unmanifest, on their own terms.

But here's the part most people miss: It wasn't Krishna who dissolved her. It was her longing.

Devotion's true magic isn't in having your love reciprocated. It's in loving without condition, reward, or destination. It's in yearning for something that will never be yours in the conventional sense —because the 'you' doing the wanting must disappear for union to happen. That's the real alchemy of devotion: The longing grows so intense and pure that it burns through the illusion of the separate self. You don't get what you want. You *become* it.

We've been conditioned to believe that trust is risky, surrender is weak, and devotion is outdated. But Bhakti turns that upside down. It's the PhD of soul evolution and the highest intelligence there is.

Because it's not a trick of the intellect; it's the collapse of the ego—a full-body, full-soul surrender to the divine, even when it doesn't answer your prayers or meet your expectations. Especially then.

Anyone can argue, and anyone can win a debate, but it takes a whole different level of strength to lose. It takes courage to kneel, radical acceptance to let go of everything the mind clings to, and to whisper, 'I trust', into the void.

Mirabai didn't care what they called her: Mad in love, obsessed, or downright crazy. She was too busy being free. And that's the final joke of devotion.

Solulu 2

Accept Appearing Foolish

Let's be honest. Half of human suffering isn't about pain—it's about looking stupid.

We don't fear ignorance. We fear appearing ignorant at the dinner table where someone mentions Murakami and you're stuck wondering if it's some exotic sushi. This is the disease of superiority: That deep, compulsive itch to be the smartest, most informed, most spiritually evolved person in the room—or at least the group chat.

See, we're all stitched from the same cosmic cloth. Nobody's better or worse. Everyone—good, bad, divine, or delulu—is a character played by consciousness, designed to mirror you back to yourself. The moment you stop cutting that cloth into good vs bad, right vs wrong, woke vs asleep, and start loving the entire fabric—frays and all. You begin to experience unity, not as a philosophical idea, but as a living, breathing truth.

Each time you feel the urge to judge someone, pause. Observe the inner reaction. What belief, bias, wound, or borrowed opinion is driving it? Because here's the quiet truth: Every judgment is a confession. What you can't tolerate in someone else is often the very thing you're still disowning in yourself.

The attack you think you're launching outward is really a missed opportunity to look inward. So, flip that judgement inward. And if you pay attention to the noise in your mind, you'll notice it's not about them at all. It's your ego, thirsty for validation, trying to prove you're smarter, better, righter. Let it go.

True intelligence isn't about being clever. It's about being empty and not needing to dominate. Real intelligence doesn't care if it's right. It simply sees. And in that seeing, the need to judge starts to dissolve. The voice shifts from *I know better* to *Hmm. I am learning so much by just witnessing this.*

There's a big difference between being woke and being awake. Woke is loud, self-righteous, and obsessed with cancel culture. Awake is quiet, curious, and too busy cleaning its own karmic lint to worry about yours. Awakening isn't about collecting spiritual merit badges. It's about realising you know far less than you thought . . . and still choosing to show up with humility. It's going from 'I have an opinion' to 'I need to sit with this.'

Here's the truth: We're all stupid. Every one of us. It doesn't matter how many degrees you have, how many self-help books you've devoured, or how many ayahuasca trips you've experienced. If you're still judging, still needing to be right, still performing your identity like a well-rehearsed TED Talk, you're not free.

The path to Shiva, 'that which is not', isn't about becoming someone special. It's about dropping everything you're not: The roles, narratives, and curated self-image. It's about becoming absolutely nothing. Because only in that radical emptiness—*Shunya* (zero)—can the real intelligence of the universe touch you.

Delulu 3

MY BELIEF IS THE TRUTH

'What one man calls "God", another calls "The Law of Physics".'

- Nikola Tesla

The Bubble of Belief

Religion is that one party guest no one really wants to invite, but everyone ends up discussing by dessert. It has single-handedly caused more wars, more divorces, and more WhatsApp family-group exits than any other topic in human history. One wrong word and suddenly you are the Antichrist, or worse, unfollowed.

Everyone is so terrified of offending someone's beliefs that we tiptoe around the subject as though walking through a minefield in clown shoes. But the thing about certainty, whether painted with a cross or wrapped in logic, is that it is a barrier to truth—not belief or disbelief, but the exhausting human obsession with being right.

The atheist and the theist are spiritual twins separated at birth, both clinging to their version of 'what is', both allergic to the phrase 'I don't know'. The atheist places faith in facts, the theist in faith itself. Both are too busy building their sandcastles of belief to notice that the tide doesn't care.

Meanwhile, the seeker is not here to debate. The seeker watches the sunrise with goosebumps, thinking, 'There's definitely something going on here . . . but I don't need to name it.' The seeker understands what both sides miss: Certainty is a comfort blanket we wrap around the unknown, but it doesn't make us warm; it simply makes us stubborn.

I did not arrive at this realisation through blind belief, philosophy or psychedelics. I arrived there through a good old-fashioned identity crisis.

My mother was born Hindu and converted to Christianity as a teenager—the kind of Christian who believed idol worship would send you straight to Satan's VIP lounge.

My father, born a Hindu, too, went in the opposite direction and declared himself an atheist. The only thing they agreed on was that we children would be raised Christian. That was the dealbreaker for my mother: No Jesus, no marriage. My father shrugged and said, 'Sure,' probably because he thought we would all grow out of it.

So, there I was, a brown Christian child, growing up in Singapore, munching on Bible stories, church camps, and Sunday school. I had more 'Jesus Loves Me' stickers than a Hillsong gift shop. Praise and worship were not simply activities; they were my emotional-support playlist. When I felt neglected or invisible, I would close my eyes, sing hymns as though they were love songs, and convince myself that even if no one else saw me, 'Jesus loved me', and that kept me from collapsing.

As I grew older and life grew messier, that love began to feel one-sided. Where was He when things went wrong, when I prayed and nothing changed? Slowly, my reverence curdled into resentment, and I drifted, one unanswered prayer at a time.

We moved to Gujarat in 1998. There, my grandmother maintained a full-blown relationship with Lord Krishna: She bathed him, dressed him, and talked to him as though he were her partner. I found it wildly fascinating. Honestly, it looked like an elaborate version of playing with dolls, something at which I already excelled. When I tried to participate, my mother pulled me aside and whispered with grave Protestant horror, 'We don't worship idols.'

That was my first moment of religious dissonance. Why would a loving God deny a child the joy of dressing a blue man in sequins? Why would He even find it offensive?

My confusion deepened when we moved to Mumbai and I entered a convent school purely because I had checked the right religion box. On my first day of Year 8, Sister Babitha—my class teacher and a nun of the Franciscan Missionaries of Mary—peered at the vacant 'Religion' column in my diary and asked, 'What is your religion, girlie?'

Freshly thirteen and newly rebellious, I looked her straight in the eye and said, 'I don't know.' She blinked. I blinked. And just like that, she became an eternal witness to my spiritual evolution over the next two decades.

Meanwhile, my father had started to dabble in spirituality, owing to a local guru my grandparents were following. I suspect it was less spiritual curiosity and more midlife existential dread, but one day he announced that we were doing the *Chardham Yatra*, the holiest of Hindu pilgrimages, across the Himalayas.

To everyone's surprise, my mother agreed. 'I just love the mountains,' she said, as if the Himalayas were neutral territory and not Shiva's backyard. Off we went: A Protestant Christian, an atheist surgeon, and me—a pubescent girl hoping for a free holiday. My sister, on the other hand, decided to sit this one out in Mumbai. She preferred having the house to herself for three weeks.

The pilgrimage was utter chaos. I suffered meltdowns about an entire state being vegetarian. I was barred from entering the Gangotri Temple because I was on my period. I could not, for the life of me, understand why people were throwing plastic into rivers that were considered goddesses. Yet I still woke at 3 a.m. in 0°C and attended the ritual at Kedarnath Temple barefoot. Why? Curiosity . . . and FOMO!

My father returned claiming he had had a mystical experience, while all I had seen were a bunch of noisy, bare-chested men smearing a rock with dairy products. What I did not return with was a belief system—and *that* was the beginning of everything real.

Believing to Seeking

By the time we settled into our Mumbai routine, church had quietly faded from our weekly schedule. My mother, who had always craved a sense of meaning beyond Sunday sermons, came across a newspaper photograph of a man who looked like Jesus if he had been dipped in filter coffee and handed a turban.

Something about him jogged her memory. She had seen him years earlier, when he was offering a programme called 'Inner Engineering'. She had wanted to attend but could not, because school pickups and meal logistics had taken priority. Now, seven years later, here he was again, in the right place at the right time.

She persuaded my father to sign up with her. He went reluctantly but returned behaving as though he had joined a cult of salad-eaters. Overnight, onions, garlic, and meat vanished from their diet. I was horrified. First, they took my mother's chicken curry; then they came for my logic.

Within months, our house was filled with books and DVDs of this man called 'Sadhguru'—or, as I sarcastically christened him,

'Sad-Guru'. I fought back with my only weapon: Debate. If school had taught me how to argue, I intended to argue.

Two years of this spiritual turf war passed. In the quiet spaces between arguments, something shifted: My questions deepened. I found myself snooping through their ever-growing library, hunting for holes in his philosophy, hoping to uncover a scam. Instead, I stumbled upon *Mystic's Musings*. To my surprise, I rather liked it. He made sense—too much sense—and that was inconvenient for my teenage pride.

Still convinced that Inner Engineering was a cleverly disguised placebo, I signed up for the course in 2009, determined to expose it from within. The teachers seemed like obvious knock-offs of Sadhguru, mimicking his voice and hand gestures like spiritual impersonators; I could not take it seriously. I wanted the original, not a low-budget remake. So, I dropped out on the condition that I would only learn if he personally taught me.

The following year, Sadhguru himself was scheduled to teach a five-day retreat called 'The Inner Way' at the Isha Yoga Centre, set in the lush foothills of the Velliangiri Mountains. My mother lit up like Diwali and offered me a place. I accepted, seeing it as a once-in-a-lifetime chance to observe him in his natural habitat and, perhaps, pull the curtain back on the wizard.

We were practically living in his armpit for those five days. One session remains lodged in my memory. He asked the room which one of these statements was true:

1. I am the body and mind.
2. The body and mind are mine.
3. I am not the body and mind, and neither are they mine.

I selected Option 1, loud and proud, and was promptly summoned to play the role of class idiot.

'What is your name?' he asked.

'Natasha,' I replied, with the full sass of a 19-year-old know-it-all. (The 'J' was yet to make an appearance in my name.)

He proceeded. 'If you lose one arm, are you still Natasha?'

'Yes.'

'And if you lose the other arm?'

That was when the light bulb went off, but it was too late. I was already ensnared.

Reluctantly, I answered, 'Yes.'

Sadhguru meticulously deconstructed my entire concept of body and mind, right up to the question, 'If you go into a coma, are you still Natasha?'

By the end, I had walked straight into his philosophical trap. I could not help admiring the way he dismantled my argument—not to win, but to show how flimsy the whole structure was to begin with. He was funny, warm, sharp, and annoyingly likeable. I still remained sceptical about his talk of 'consciousness', but I began to suspect he might be more than mere spiritual clickbait.

I returned home and, out of sheer stubbornness, committed to the twenty-one-minute daily Inner Engineering practice of stretches, breathing, and chanting. I did it not because I believed in it, but because I hoped to disprove it. The joke was on me.

I had assumed spirituality would feel like peace and floating through life in white robes on a fluffy cloud. Instead, it performed a brutal demolition job. Over the next four years, everything to which I had clung—my beliefs, opinions, ideology, and sense of identity—was shredded. Then, at twenty-two, the man I thought was my happy-ever-after ghosted me as though I had never existed, and my whole inner world crumbled.

My parents invited me to another event at the Isha Yoga Centre: Three days of discourses with Sadhguru. Although I had not, in those five years, had a single experience in his presence, I found entertainment in his wisdom, so I accepted the invitation.

When you hit rock bottom, there is no escaping into the future or bargaining with the past. There is only the unbearable immediacy of now. Sometimes that is where the magic happens. And it did.

It was the final session on the final day when Sadhguru, in all his mystical grandeur, performed his signature thunderous clap. In that moment, an electric current bolted up my spine and detonated between my brows. For the first time, I saw him not as the man I had labelled 'Sad-Guru', but as Buddha, Krishna, or Jesus sitting in front of me.

I collapsed into uncontrollable sobs as all my judgements, intellectual arrogance, and spiritual sarcasm melted away. That day, Sadhguru ceased to be spiritual entertainment and became my guru.

Here is the most beautiful part: He never tried to convert me. He did not ask for my belief or my obedience. He asked only that I remain open and continue seeking. In doing so, he returned to me the one thing I did not know I had lost: Myself.

Dispeller of Darkness

'Guru' literally means the 'dispeller of darkness'. A real guru doesn't slide into your life to comfort you. In fact, it is quite the opposite: they walk in, look around at the mess you have called 'self', and say, 'All right, let us burn it all down.'

They are not here to make you feel special. They are here to challenge your comfort zone, dismantle your beliefs, and kindly—sometimes not-so-kindly—show you what a cosmic clown you have been. A true guru doesn't pamper or validate your personality. They expose the nonsense with which you have been identifying and dare you to let it go.

That is why people often resist them.

History is full of examples. Humanity meets a mystic, feels unsettled, and either persecutes them, drives them away, or reduces them to a symbol that can be safely revered without requiring any real change.

A real guru will never ask you to believe. They will ask you to see the madness of your mind and the stories it spins. And seeing that is the first step to dissolving it.

This is why Sanatan Dharma is often understood to encourage finding a living teacher. Because the moment a guru leaves the body, things can become complicated. Interpretations creep in, egos rise, communities fracture, and before you know it, teachings are codified, translated, and taught like corporate compliance training.

Consider what happened with Jesus: One man, one message; 2,000 years later, tens of thousands of denominations. Buddhism, too, branched into Theravada, Mahayana, Vajrayana, and more. Islam developed into Shia, Sunni, and other schools of thought.

Even modern spiritual paths are not immune. After Maharishi Mahesh Yogi (known as the Beatles' guru), the Transcendental Meditation organisation faced disputes, lawsuits, and leadership challenges. Yogananda's Self-Realisation Fellowship experienced internal divisions. Osho's movement, likewise, has continued to navigate legal and organisational complexities.

The moment the anchor leaves, everyone starts rowing in different directions.

Osho anticipated this. He told his disciples, 'If I am gone and your journey is incomplete, find a Sadhguru. That will not be a betrayal. It will be the highest form of respect.'

This is because it is not about attachment to a personality; it is about finding the right frequency.

Now, people often ask, 'How do I know who my guru is?' The unsatisfactory answer is: You don't. Not with logic or checklists. You don't choose a guru as you choose a fitness coach. It is not a decision you make. It is a silent, magnetic knowing that bypasses your intellect and goes straight to your bones.

And before you dismiss that as spiritual fluff, here is the science of it.

Everything in this universe vibrates: you, me, your cat, your confusion. When two frequencies match, they synchronise. In physics, this is called 'entrainment'; in neuroscience, 'limbic resonance'. It is why you calm down around someone grounded or feel restless around someone agitated.

A true guru holds a frequency your system has been quietly tuning itself towards for lifetimes. When your energy hits the right pitch, the guru appears in your life. You might resist; you might even dislike them at first, as I did. I rolled my eyes at every word Sadhguru spoke, argued, debated, and refused to participate. But I kept getting pulled back, like a mosquito to a bug zapper—until, finally, he zapped my ego right out of me.

The guru doesn't hand you a toolkit and say, 'Go figure.' They become the flame you sit beside. That flame warms you, lights your way, and sometimes scorches your resistance. But that is what burns away the lies and makes space for the truth.

Yes, books are beautiful. Yes, teachings can inspire. But transformation takes a living presence—not someone who once walked the earth, but someone who is walking it with you. Someone who doesn't care about being liked, followed, or praised; someone who cares only about whether you are willing to drop the drama and see what they are willing to show you.

Science of Spirituality

If there is one thing I have realised in the last fifteen years of stumbling through this grand cosmic classroom, it is this: The universe, and life, are not random chaos. They are art. They are maths. They are music. They are a mystery. And they are oddly in sync with what ancient Indian yogis were mumbling about in loincloths long before lab coats became a thing.

What I admire about science is that it is essentially a fastidious seeker. It pokes, it prods, it double-checks its homework. Sure, it can be a bit of a control freak, running around chasing its own tail, but every now and then it trips over a truth so wild it ends up sounding like something a rishi in the Himalayas would have said mid-trance.

Take the speed of light. The *Surya Siddhanta*, an astronomical text written thousands of years ago, describes light as travelling 2,202 *yojanas* in half a *nimesha*, which, when converted, comes to roughly 1,85,793 miles per second. Modern science, armed with satellites and space lasers, clocks it at 1,86,282. That's a margin of just 0.26 per cent. Even if exact conversions can be debated, you have to admit—that level of cosmic math from an ancient text makes 'advanced civilisation' feel like a relative term.

Then there is the number 108, sacred in yoga, mantra, mala beads and temple architecture. It turns out that the diameter of the Sun multiplied by 108 equals the distance between the Earth and the Sun. The same goes for the Moon.

The ancients did not arrive at these insights by mapping galaxies. They looked inward. They treated the human body as a laboratory and consciousness as the microscope. It was as if they thought, 'If I can crack the code of this body, perhaps I will understand the blueprint of the entire universe.'

Here is another example: We take about fifteen breaths a minute, which works out to around 21,600 breaths per day. The circumference of the Earth at the equator is also 21,600 nautical miles. The numerical parallel makes for a poetic way to imagine our breath in rhythm with the planet's geometry.

My favourite crossover episode between science and spirituality is the origin story.

In yogic lore, the origin of everything begins with Shiva—the still, silent backdrop of existence. He is not doing anything. He is not even being anything. He is just there. Or rather, not-there: A living embodiment of no-thingness. Darkness, silence, and void. The kind of stillness so complete it makes outer space look busy.

Then Shakti enters: Fierce, electric, and bursting with energy. She is the movement that longs to dance, the light that wants to shine and the force that refuses to sit still. She looks at Shiva, sleeping, and decides it is time to wake him.

At first, he ignores her. He is quite content being inert. But she persists, and eventually she manages to wake him. And, like anyone forced awake from deep sleep, Shiva lets out a primal *roar*, from which, apparently, creation emerged.

What follows is a dance. Shiva and Shakti move in rhythm, in sync, in wild divine intimacy. And through their dance, the entire universe unfolds.

Sounds poetic, does it not? But wait, science says something eerily similar. In physics, for example, a vacuum state (Shiva) gives rise to an electromagnetic field (Shakti), which produces virtual pairs of particles (a kind of cosmic dance of Shiva and Shakti). When the field is strong enough, those virtual particles become real matter and antimatter. It may be an analogy, but it is hard not to notice the resonance.

The yogis were not scribbling equations. They were sitting still and watching—tuning in so deeply to the nature of existence that they perceived what physicists would later discover with billion-dollar machines.

The parallels don't end there. Science speaks of the Big Bang, a singular event that set everything into motion. In yogic lore, creation doesn't happen just once. It rises and dissolves in cycles. There is not one bang; there are many. It is an ongoing rhythm of expansion and contraction—inhale, exhale.

Sadhguru once related a story about meeting the American physicist Paul Steinhardt, co-author of the book *Endless Universe*. At a conference, he asked Paul, 'Is it possible that it was not a bang but a roar, a continuous roar?' (Sadhguru 2020)

Paul paused, intrigued, and suggested that it is indeed possible. Sadhguru then smiled and said, 'Someday if your research takes you there, keep this as a guide point. He has roared eighty-four times.'

Paul, being a scientist, asked the obvious question: 'How do you know?'

Sadhguru replied, 'By looking into my system, I am saying that creation has roared eighty-four times and it will roar further, many more times.' He further added that when a tree is cut, its rings reveal a history of events such as droughts, heavy rain, or fires over the past thousand years. In the same way, if you examine the human system with awareness, you'll find it holds the entire history of its development. This creation has gone through its cycle eighty-four times.

It is a bold claim. But it doesn't ask for blind belief. It invites you to look inward, not outward. Just as tree rings record every season, the human system, when observed with clarity, holds memory beyond biology. Awareness, it turns out, is the microscope. Or perhaps the telescope.

Holy Trinity

There is something about the number three that the universe simply cannot get over. It shows up everywhere like some divine inside joke that has been playing for millennia. Every major tradition has its own version of a cosmic trio.

Christianity has the *Father*, the *Son*, and the *Holy Spirit*. Hinduism—never one to keep things minimal—gives us *Brahma* the creator, *Vishnu* the preserver, and *Shiva* the destroyer.

Now here's where it gets fun. It turns out that modern science also follows the rule of three. Everything around us, from the chair you're sitting on to the thoughts in your head, is made of atoms. And what are atoms made of? Protons, neutrons, and electrons. Another holy trinity! Coincidence? Possibly. But maybe it's more than that.

Let us break it down.

Protons are the positive ones. They form the heart of the atom and sound suspiciously like Brahma, the creator. Neutrons are neutral; they don't pick sides. They simply hang out in the middle, quietly doing the work of keeping everything stable. That's Vishnu energy right there: The ultimate cosmic maintenance man. And then we have electrons. Negative in charge, full of energy, constantly zipping around in unpredictable orbits. That's Shiva to a tee. The rebel. The transformer. The one who keeps things from getting too comfortable.

Who is making all this movement possible? Enter *Shakti* or *Devi*. In yogic lore, she's the divine feminine force, the energy that animates all creation. In atomic terms, she's the electromagnetic force. Without her, electrons would just sit still, and atoms would stop being atoms. Just as Shiva without Shakti is pure potential but no movement, the atom without the electromagnetic force is basically a paperweight. Nothing happens.

Let us hop over to Christianity for a second. Protons, with their foundational presence and positive charge, could easily represent the Father, the source. Neutrons, with their balancing, mediating role, reflect the Christ energy, the bridge between divinity and humanity. And the Holy Spirit? That is your electron. You could even say Mother Mary is like the unseen hand that keeps the system together: Gentle, essential, and often overlooked.

Here is the part that really cracked me up.

As a child, I was absolutely hopeless at science. Physics made me want to cry, and maths felt like a foreign language spoken only by calculators. Now I look back and wonder if I would have paid a bit more attention if someone had just said, 'Hey, the atom is basically Shiva doing the Tandav.' Clearly, the sages were explaining physics in metaphor. Instead, I was stuck memorising formulas with zero emotional payoff.

In the end, what blows my mind isn't just that ancient wisdom and modern science overlap. It is that they are practically flirting with each other—both attempting to explain the same mystery: What is this existence made of, and how on earth does it work?

Sounds as Keys

Some truths don't need explaining. They just hum through your bones.

Take '*AUM*,' for instance. Three little letters, one big cosmic punch. Yes, it's something you hear at the end of yoga class, just before everyone rolls up their mats and checks their phones. But this ancient sound is not merely a new-age parting gift. It is a key to the very structure of consciousness itself.

Funnily enough, most of the world's religions seem to agree: Aum. Aumen. Aumeen. Coincidence? Doubtful. More like a cosmic breadcrumb trail left behind by those who figured out that sound is not just something you hear; it's something you are.

In the yogic tradition, AUM is not chanted merely for vibes. It is the original frequency: The sound of creation. But it's not just 'Om' as many of us mumble with glazed eyes. It is 'Aaaa', 'Uuuu', and 'Mmmm'—three distinct sounds, three states of consciousness.

'A' is the waking state.
'U' is the dream or subconscious state.
'M' is the deep-sleep or unconscious state.

Here is the clever part. This primordial password to existence is the only sound that can be uttered without involving the tongue. 'A' starts with the mouth wide open. Slowly, the shape of the mouth changes and 'U' naturally flows out. Finally, when the lips meet, 'M' lands softly like the full stop at the end of a cosmic sentence. Together, they are like the RGB of sound: Everything you perceive, from the buzz of a bumblebee to Bach's cello suites, is just a remix of this original chord.

But it doesn't stop at mysticism. Science, too, has started tuning in. Everything in the universe is vibration. And where there is vibration, there is sound. Nada Yoga, the yoga of sound, explores this with the precision of a physicist and the devotion of a poet.

This is where Sanskrit strides in with quiet swagger. Unlike most languages that fumbled their way into meaning over time, Sanskrit was not invented; it was discovered. A language whose sounds are said to mirror the very vibrations of creation itself. Each syllable, when spoken with awareness, is like striking the tuning fork of the particles that make up existence.

In this paradigm, mantras are not merely background music for incense-lit rooms. They are precision tools and energy codes. These words don't just mean something; they do something. Chant them properly, and you can rewire your entire nervous system like a cosmic electrician.

So, here we are again: Ancient yogis meditating in Himalayan caves, decoding the cosmos through breath and stillness, and modern scientists poking atoms and studying frequency fields. Same song, different instruments.

INGREDIENTS OF CREATION

If AUM is the sound that launched the universe, then what came next?

The ingredients of creation.

This is where another mantra quietly steps into the spotlight, carrying the weight of millennia on its five syllables:

Na-Ma-Shi-Va-Ya.

This is not just another spiritual chant to try under a full moon. It's what's called the *Maha Mantra* (in Shaiva traditions)—the mantra of all mantras. Just as Shiva is regarded as *Mahadev*, the God of Gods, this is considered the foundational chant in yogic traditions.

Each syllable corresponds to one of the five elements: *Na* represents Earth, *Ma* is Water, *Shi* stands for Fire, *Va* is Air, and *Ya* signifies Space. Everything that exists in the physical world, including you, is made up of just these five ingredients. These elements are the building blocks of your inner cosmos. As Jesus so simply put it, 'The Kingdom of God is within you.' He wasn't only being metaphorical.

Now, because Jesus was my Lord and Saviour at one point—and praise and worship used to be my emotional support playlist—when I was back in Singapore for my undergraduate studies, my coping mechanism shapeshifted into listening to Shiva chants on loop.

Maybe because he never promised to answer my prayers or save me. He didn't ghost me with divine promises I couldn't understand. He was simply the God of Destruction. Honestly, that felt more real, and strangely, it made me feel more seen.

My personal favourite chant was the *Panchakshara Stotram,* built around the Maha Mantra. I had no clue what it meant, but *Aum Namah Shivaya* rolled off my tongue as if it had been sitting there all along. At the time, it was just a vibe. I didn't realise I was essentially inviting the Lord of Cosmic Destruction into my life on repeat.

Then, in 2017, I stumbled upon a video of Sadhguru very casually telling people to be careful before chanting 'Aum Namah Shivaya', because this wasn't your average spiritual sedative; it was the equivalent of handing Shiva your house keys, your emotional attachments, and your carefully curated personality, and saying, 'Cool, go ahead, do your thing. Destroy.'

Oops!

No wonder things had started crumbling. Relationships that once felt unshakeable began to crack open. Illusions I had clung to like security blankets got yanked away. The people I thought I loved started revealing their fine print. Turns out, Shiva's idea of a good time is showing you everything you've been conveniently avoiding.

That's the thing about mantras: You don't have to understand them for them to work. Sometimes your soul knows what it needs long before your mind gets the memo. I finally got it: Shiva was there to burn the nonsense, and 'Aum Namah Shivaya' was the matchstick.

Over time, I began to understand what exactly I was really tuning into.

> *Na*, the grounding weight of Earth.
> *Ma*, the fluid surrender of Water.
> *Shi*, the purifying burn of Fire.
> *Va*, the invisible momentum of Air.
> *Ya*, the spacious silence of Space.

In yoga, there's a process called *Bhuta Shuddhi*, or the purification of the five elements. Yogis say that when you gain mastery over your inner elements, life stops being a struggle. You stop arguing with reality because your perception becomes crystal clear.

One of the most visceral expressions of this elemental awe is the Ganga Aarti. If you've ever stood on the banks of the Ganges at dusk, watching the flames rise while bells clash and voices call out to the sky, you'll know what I mean. It's not a religious ritual; it's an elemental love song—fire rising to greet the heavens, air vibrating with sound, water flowing with purpose, earth supporting, and space embracing it in stillness.

It doesn't matter what religion you follow. The Ganga Aarti moves you because it speaks in a language older than words: The ingredients that built the universe . . . and all of us.

Soon, it dawned on me that the reason I drifted away from the religion I once knew was because it merely gave me a name for God. The elements gave me a way to feel God.

TEMPLES AS TECHNOLOGY

In Sanatan Dharma, there's no single cosmic CEO. Instead, everything is seen as sacred. The river is sacred. The sun is sacred. The breeze that flips your hair on a Sunday afternoon? Sacred. Each element of nature holds its own godhood not because we needed extra names in our mythology, but because the ancients saw life pulsing through every form.

So then, why temples?

If God is everywhere, why squeeze into a crowded sanctum, elbowing aunties and dodging coconuts just to catch a glimpse of a deity? Why not pray to a pothole on your way to work?

Because temples aren't about begging or bargaining with God. They're about transformation. Built with the precision of sacred geometry and powered by energies you can't see but can absolutely feel, temples function more like inner-alignment stations. You don't come here to outsource your spirituality; you come to get in tune.

This wasn't some whimsical setup either. Temples followed the *Agama Shastras*—an ancient manual of architecture, energy placement, geometry, and sacred rituals. Every angle, every stone, every chant was crafted to interact with the subtle layers of your being. And right at the heart of it all is the *Vigraha*, the idol. Except it's not just a symbolic statue; it's a living, vibrating energy form.

Now, you may ask, how is this stone a living thing? Enter *Prana Pratishtha*. A skilled practitioner who has mastered their own energy body channels their life force into the idol, 'programming' it with a specific vibration.

If this sounds far-fetched, think about it in modern terms. If physics tells us that matter can store and transmit energy, it's a useful analogy for what the ancients may have intuited. The statue becomes a kind of energy transformer, connecting you to a broader, subtler field of consciousness.

For years, I wondered why those priests in Kedarnath were so determined to drench that rock with dairy products. Turns out, there's a method to that madness, too.

Certain materials, like granite or quartz, have piezoelectric properties. When liquids such as milk, ghee, and honey—known to enhance the flow of prana—are poured over the rock, it creates mechanical stress, generating a subtle electric charge. That charge interacts with your energy body when you touch or meditate near the idol. And when you consume the remnants, or *Prasadam*, you're literally ingesting some of that energy.

Ancient wisdom? Absolutely. But also, physics. And we're not done yet. Temples have more tricks up their sleeve. Their design incorporates resonance. When mantras are chanted or bells are rung, the sound waves interact with the temple's architecture, creating vibrations that ripple through the space. The resonance amplifies the energy emanating from the rock, forming a field that can subtly sync with your nervous system.

If you've ever walked into a temple and suddenly felt shaky, tearful, or as though you've plugged into something you can't quite explain, that's not random. That's resonance again—the temple's energy meeting your energy, and something shifting.

And if your *Kundalini* decides to wake up in that moment, well . . . good luck walking out the same person who walked in! When that raw life force at the base of your spine stirs, it's not subtle. It's like plugging a five-watt bulb into a high-voltage socket. Your energy body kicks into overdrive, and suddenly that statue isn't just a statue; it's a doorway to something far greater.

Even the daily rituals at temples—the fire offerings, the water libations, the chanting—aren't just ceremonial flourishes. They serve a purpose. Every action is about keeping the temple 'charged', maintaining its connection to the elements: Earth, water, fire, air, and, most importantly, ether.

And there's that magical ingredient. *Ether* acts as a bridge between the physical and the divine. Without it, the temple is just a beautiful building. But with it, you've got a portal.

The Infinite Void

If Earth is your body, Water your blood, Fire your metabolism, and Air your breath, then Space—or Ether—is everything in between. It's the vast, invisible field that holds it all together. In yogic science, this element is called *Akasha*, and it governs our ability to communicate with clarity and truth. It's what makes mantras work, prayers heard, and silence speak louder than words ever could.

Here's a fun fact: Fire and Ether are two elements that are deeply connected. Fire is said to generate an etheric field around the flame—an energy bubble that amplifies our connection to the subtle realms. That's why every culture, from the Vikings to the Vedas to your grandma's altar, incorporates fire rituals. The flame, quite literally, becomes a hotline to the divine. And if you've ever sat around a campfire or enjoyed a candlelit dinner, you'll know the magic I'm referring to.

While science discarded the old 'aether' theory, quantum physics now hints that emptiness isn't truly empty. The Quantum Vacuum is a void teeming with virtual particles and subtle energy fluctuations—a seething soup of potential that gives rise to all matter. If that's not Akasha in a lab coat, I don't know what is.

If you zoom into an atom, you'll find it's more void than substance. Over 99.9999 per cent of it is just space. Even the tiny bits we call 'particles' are really waves of probability dancing in emptiness. That same emptiness makes up over 99 per cent of the observable universe. Which raises the question: If everything is mostly nothing, what exactly is this 'nothing'?

Here's where the ancient yogis had a head start. They didn't call it 'nothing'; in Shaiva philosophy, they called it Shiva. Okay, I get it! We've thrown a lot of metaphors at you. Shiva is the *Destroyer*, Shiva is the *Adiyogi*, Shiva is the *electron*, Shiva is the *void*, Shiva is *no-thing*. So, who or what exactly is this Shiva?

Let's clear it up.

Shiva isn't a person. He's not some caveman figure brooding on a Himalayan mountaintop with a snake around his neck. Shiva is a principle. A state. The unmanifest intelligence that both holds and dissolves form. When we say Shiva is the electron, we mean he's the energy spinning inside matter. When we say Shiva is the void, the no-thing, we mean he's the stillness behind all movement. When we say he's the destroyer, he's the destroyer of illusions. When we say Adiyogi, we mean the first one (perhaps an alien) who knew this and decided to share the cheat codes with humanity.

Shiva is the dance and the stillness, the chaos and the calm; the nothing that is everything. He's not judging your karma or your dessert choices. He is the dessert, the craving, and even the void you tried to fill with it.

Which brings us to the part you've probably felt but never had words for.

There's a space inside you that nothing ever really fills. You've tried relationships, promotions, green juice, one more scroll through

Instagram, but something in you still feels . . . hollow. And sometimes, that void inside scares you.

But what if that space isn't emptiness? What if it's sacred?

That deep, quiet pocket inside you *is* Shiva. That's the blueprint of the divine. What felt like absence is actually presence. You're not lacking; you're limitless.

This is the ultimate cosmic prank. The thing we've been trying to escape is actually the thing we *are*. Because when you stop running from it and sit with it long enough to hear the silence whisper back, you'll realise that the void was not the problem; it was the portal!

You don't need to fill the void. You need to become it. Because when you become it, you don't disappear. You expand.

Solulu 3

Make Peace with Uncertainty

We love the idea of certainty. It feels safe, stable, and warm. It's like tucking yourself into a bed where nothing unexpected ever happens. But certainty doesn't actually bring peace. It brings rigidity. And rigidity? That's the fast lane to suffering.

Our obsession with knowing what's coming, what's right, and what's real is almost always about control. We want life to behave. We want it to follow a script we wrote in our heads, preferably in neat bullet points with no surprise endings. But life doesn't read your script. It doesn't care for your plot twists or your carefully laid plans. It just happens. And the more we try to grip it, the more it slips through our fingers.

The truth is, certainty is an illusion.

One of the sneakiest ways this need for control shows up is in the form of beliefs. We cling to ideologies, religions, opinions, and moral codes like lifeboats in a stormy sea. But most of the time, we're not defending truth. We're defending our egos because arguing over who's right is fundamentally about soothing our sense of self-worth.

Now, instead of going to war over whose truth is truer, what if we softened? What if we listened curiously, not defensively? Because when we listen like that, with our hearts and not just our rebuttals ready, we start seeing the overlaps. We start recognising that under the surface, we're all more alike than we think.

Letting go of the need to be right or certain doesn't mean becoming apathetic or flaky. It means becoming available to new perspectives—to learning, to growing, to being wrong, and sometimes spectacularly so. But still being okay with it. You stop treating life like a puzzle to be solved and start experiencing it like the mystery it's meant to be.

And if you're genuinely curious about discovering the source of creation, look inward. Every mystic has said the same thing in different ways: God is not out there, hiding behind a cloud. God is within you.

The ultimate plot twist is that even the most awakened beings don't know it all. Not even close. What sets them apart is that they've emptied themselves of beliefs, opinions, conditioning, projections, and mental clutter. They live in a kind of inner stillness where perception is clear, not clouded by the need to be right. From that clarity, they can learn anything. They can study, experiment, and experience. But even then, to know everything would still take a few million lifetimes.

So, the next time you feel the itch to prove a point, dominate a discussion, or flaunt your spiritual GPA, remember this: Nobody has it all figured out. Not the saints. Not the scientists. Not even you with your colour-coded tabs in your NIV Study Bible.

That's not a flaw in the system. That is the system. So maybe, just relax.

Delulu 4

I AM A GOOD PERSON

'I have never seen a greater monster
or miracle than myself.'
- Michel De Montaigne

Lack OSX

Once upon a time, in a Pinterest-perfect garden, lived Adam and Eve, the original poster children for the minimalist lifestyle. Eden was an all-inclusive paradise with perpetually ripe fruit, perfect weather, and absolutely zero mosquitoes. Body positivity wasn't a movement; it was just life: Naked, unashamed, and vibing with God on the daily.

Then one day, while Adam was off naming animals—and possibly regretting 'platypus'—the serpent slid into Eve's DMs with the finesse of a late-night thirst trap. 'Hey, girl. That fruit God told you not to touch? It's a limited edition. One bite and you'll unlock the cheat codes to the universe.'

Maybe she was bored with endless paradise, maybe she was curious, or maybe she just needed a little chaos. Either way, she clicked the link. And just like that, 'shame' installed itself like a shady virus from a fake giveaway site.

One second, they're chilling like that CEO and HR lady at a concert, and the next? Exposed on Coldplay's Kiss Cam, scrambling for cover, grabbing the nearest fig leaves, and diving into bushes, launching humanity's longest-running multiplayer game: Hide from God.

When confronted, Adam did what men have done ever since—he blamed the woman. Eve wasn't having it either, so she blamed the snake. Thus, blame-shifting quietly became the default setting on humanity's operating system.

But here is the part religion rarely pauses to examine.

If God created *everything*, then the serpent wasn't a bug in the system—it was part of the code. Because let's be real: If humans were never meant to touch that fruit, why even make it? Why put it right in the middle? That's not just temptation, that's UX design begging for a click.

All creation runs on duality—just like the binary code: 0 and 1. Absence and presence. Off and on. Stillness and movement. Shiva and Shakti. Masculine and feminine. Every system, from cosmic expansion to computer logic, functions because of polarity. Even Christianity echoes it: 'The Word' and 'The Breath'—two sides of one divine algorithm.

When you see it through that lens, the serpent's role stops looking evil and starts looking essential. Eve wasn't seduced by sin; she was stirred by curiosity, by the innate drive of consciousness to know itself. That bite is what created the contrast. Because to know light, you have to meet darkness. To know God, you must first experience separation.

Older goddess-centred civilisations understood this. They didn't see the serpent as the villain. The Egyptians crowned their pharaohs with the cobra for divine authority. The Greeks gave their god of healing, *Asclepius*, a serpent staff—a symbol so powerful, it's still used in medicine. The Mesoamericans revered *Quetzalcoatl*, the feathered serpent god of wisdom. In India, Vishnu reclines on the cosmic serpent, *Sheshanaga*. Shiva wears *Vasuki* like jewellery. Even the dormant consciousness at the base of your spine is called *Kundalini*—a coiled serpent waiting to rise. The same serpent that was feared across the world was honoured as the conduit between heaven and earth.

So, what if the 'fall' was never a fall?

It is more likely that the bite was the first spark of consciousness, saying, 'Wait, who am I?' It was the beginning of awareness, individuality, longing, and choice—the foundations of what we now call 'free will'.

The serpent didn't tempt humanity into sin; it initiated humanity into awareness. God didn't exile them from paradise; He expanded it. Because what good is bliss if you don't know you're in it?

Monotheism couldn't handle the paradox of duality, so it split creation into a black and white—'God' and 'Satan'. And because patriarchy needed a villain, Eve became the prototype for every woman who dared to question authority, follow her curiosity, or listen to her own body. The code was rewritten to teach obedience instead of insight, guilt over intuition.

The irony is that we've been living in that same patchy code ever since—trying to run a whole operating system on only one half of its circuitry. We worship the 'light' but fear the shadow, crave the divine but suppress the body, chase heaven but neglect the earth. No wonder humanity keeps glitching!

Now, if you think we've evolved past all the Garden of Eden business, think again, because the real apple was delivered by Steve Jobs—sleek, silver, and glowing in our palm. We didn't even need a snake; we queued up ourselves. And instead of fig leaves, we now hide behind curated identities, scroll for knowledge, shop for meaning, and trace intimacy for followers. The 'Fall' just got an upgrade.

But the lesson hasn't changed. The serpent wasn't the enemy, and the apple was never the problem. Here's the inconvenient truth: We must fall before we rise. We have to break down before we break through because destruction comes before creation.

The more you awaken, the more you realise that we're born into stories and systems we didn't choose—beliefs, fears, and rules. It's not our fault, but it's our responsibility to question them.

It starts with looking honestly at ourselves. Where did we get these ideas? Whose voices and beliefs are we still carrying around? Before we can rewrite the script, we've got to figure out which parts were never ours to begin with.

Core Memory

From the moment we tumble into this world—red-faced, howling, and utterly confused—we begin a game we never agreed to play: The game of being 'good enough'.

Think about it. You start out as this blissed-out blob of jelly, farting freely and double-chinning your way through life. You have zero concept of shame or whether your onesie matches your aura. But then, one misplaced pee outside the nappy, and suddenly the vibe changes. Eyebrows furrow. Voices tense. You've broken an unspoken rule.

That's the first download: Love is conditional.

We start logging every reaction like amateur data scientists. 'Smile = good. Cry = bad. Be cute, get cuddles. Be chaotic, get chided.' Nobody says it outright, but the memo is clear: Approval is a performance, authenticity is a risk, and emotional honesty is best kept on a leash.

Then comes kindergarten, where your weirdness goes through its first corporate rebranding. You're on the playground pretending to be a dinosaur-astronaut-princess-ninja, roaring and twirling like your life depends on it. But instead of joining the fun, your teacher gently suggests, 'Why don't you go play with the other girls?' Translation: 'Your imagination is adorable, but only within the confines of gender roles and social decorum.' You're five, and apparently already violating the dress code of acceptable reality.

By the time school rolls around, we're fully enrolled in the Shame Games. Mistakes aren't stepping stones; they're existential crises. Fail a test? Internalised as 'I'm stupid'. Get rejected by a friend group? It becomes a personality flaw. Life turns into an endless audition, and the judges are everyone you've ever wanted to impress.

Then comes puberty, that magical time when your body turns into a science experiment nobody warned you about. Suddenly, the same body that once just existed peacefully now comes with disclaimers, dress codes, and unsolicited advice. You're either too much or not enough. Too loud, too soft, too hairy, too flat, too interested, not interested enough. You're expected to be aware of your sexuality, but not *too* aware. Welcome to the 'look sexy, but don't know it' paradox.

To top it all off, sex education is often a mix of awkward metaphors, outdated diagrams, and a heavy dose of fear. Somewhere between the banana demonstrations and 'abstinence is best' sermons, we absorb the central message: Sex is dangerous. Handle it wrong, and you'll end up emotionally scarred, physically punished, or spiritually damned.

By adulthood, we're seasoned pros. We know the drill: Work hard, say the right things, don't offend anyone. The workplace is just school with better coffee and less honesty. Deadlines loom like moral judgements, promotions feel like proof of worth, and failure isn't feedback—it's a character flaw. And burnout? That's just the price of being a 'high-functioning adult'.

Then comes the ultimate minefield of 'relationships'. We drag our childhood conditioning into romance like a suitcase full of unpaid bills. We crave closeness but fear rejection. We long for intimacy but feel shame about desire. Most of us weren't taught how to talk about sex, love, or emotions, and so we assume. We mimic what we see in films, half-believing that grand gestures and perfectly timed playlists will heal our unspoken wounds.

And just when you think you've survived it all, along comes social media—the global leaderboard of insecurity. Now, it's not enough to be 'good' in real life; you've got to perform it 24x7. Scroll long enough, and you'll find someone with a better body, more zen mornings, cuter children, cleaner aesthetics, and more poetic captions. Even your dog seems underachieving by comparison.

The fear of not measuring up becomes chronic. Every selfie comes with an invisible subtitle: 'Am I enough yet?' And no matter how many likes you rack up, the guilt creeps in. 'Why can't I be more grateful? More productive? More photogenic while sipping matcha under a Sakura tree in Kyoto?'

Eventually, many of us become parents. And here, the cycle does a sneaky U-turn. Suddenly, you're the one teaching someone else how to be 'good', all while praying you're not passing down the same neuroses you swore you'd unlearn. But when you're exhausted, overwhelmed, and operating from the same blueprint you inherited, the old scripts resurface. You find yourself repeating the very phrases you once swore were unfair: 'Because I said so.' 'Stop crying.' 'Be a good boy/girl.' And, thus, the loop continues.

It's funny how all our human dysfunction boils down to just one emotion: Shame. When we don't talk openly about our needs, desires, or boundaries, it creates the perfect breeding ground for confusion, insecurity, guilt, and disconnect. And when shame creeps into our sexuality, it doesn't just make things awkward; it distorts everything.

Some people learn to hide their desires, pretending they don't exist. Others swing to the opposite extreme and use sex as a way to feel powerful or validated. That's why cheating, for example, is often just someone trying to prove to themselves that they're still desirable—still worth something.

In more harmful cases, when someone has spent their whole life feeling powerless, invisible, or worthless, they might try to reclaim control in the worst way possible: Through violence. Sexual violence, at its core, is rarely about sex; it's about control, aggression, and a warped attempt to feel strong in a world where they've always felt weak.

We are conditioned to believe that happiness, love, and success are things to be earned through effort, sacrifice, and relentless control. And so, we fall, and we keep falling until we are taught to let go of control.

Shameware

Before I became a people-pleasing, spiritual overachiever with a PhD in self-abandonment, I was just a dark, slightly demonic child with a ton of trauma and a warped moral compass.

We grew up in Singapore, in my grandfather's house, while my father was away in Germany, training to be an endoscopist. Mum worked full-time, and Grandpa did, too, which meant we were mostly left with his caretaker—a woman who clearly hadn't signed up to babysit us and was not shy about making that known. She had all the warmth of a cold-storage freezer and treated us like tiny intrusions. Every complaint to Mum about her triggered volcanic outbursts at home.

Looking back, I cannot even blame Mum. She was doing everything—working, raising two children, supporting the household financially, and receiving exactly zero emotional backup from her husband. Marriage hadn't turned out to be the fairytale she'd imagined. She was tired, frustrated and very, very alone, clinging to Jesus for hope.

We saw our father once a year, if that. When he did appear, he came under his own pressure cooker of proving his worth. So, if we did something to annoy him, out came the belt with threats about staining the walls with our blood. Mum would leap to our defence, throwing herself between us, sobbing as though she were auditioning for *Mother India*, while he tried to maintain an illusion of control through fear. Objectively, I cannot blame him either. He loved us deeply in his own way. He often made us laugh until we snorted. But emotions weren't a language he spoke. Thanks to a cocktail of generational conditioning and Amitabh Bachchan's 'Angry Young Man' era, the only emotion he had on tap was rage.

While this was occasional, our grandfather's helper resented every breath we took and served daily helpings of emotional neglect with a side of passive aggression. One evening, I must have pushed back, rebelled, or finally snapped at her cruelty. Whatever it was, it led to a massive showdown. And because I was a child and therefore belonged to Mum, the fire landed on her.

What happened next is etched into my bones. It was 2 a.m. The house had quietened, but the air was still thick with leftover fury. I don't remember anyone else being there—just Mum and me. Mum was hysterical, sobbing and inching towards the window, threatening to jump, while I clung to her nightgown, begging her not to die.

Somewhere in that tear-soaked chaos, I swallowed a message that would shape the next two decades of my life: That love was conditional, emotions were dangerous, and survival depended on performance. If I could just behave, be good enough, maybe I could keep the people I loved from leaving me.

But just as I perfected the art of emotional crowd control, life changed locations and languages.

In 1998, we moved from squeaky-clean Singapore to a small town in Gujarat where 'English-medium' education meant everyone still spoke Gujarati. I stuck out like a sore, foreign thumb. Instead of adapting, I developed a smug little superiority complex. Everything was beneath me—the food, the children, the classrooms, and the people. Especially the people.

There was a boy who lived nearby. He had done nothing wrong. He was simply dark-skinned. But my sister and I, in all our misdirected trauma and colonised thinking, mocked him and called him *Kaalia* (Gujarati for 'black'). We even hatched villainous schemes to torment him like characters in a low-budget soap opera. All because our grandmother had conditioned us that fairer was better.

Somewhere in all this damage, I was shoved into a school fancy-dress competition dressed as a silver fairy. I stepped onstage, took one look at the sea of faces, and burst into tears. The Gujarati word for fairy is '*pari*', and the word for crying is '*rari*', so the nickname '*Pari Rari*' followed me like a cursed prophecy for years. And just like that, I developed a lifelong fear of public speaking, gift-wrapped in glitter and shame.

Then came the big move to Mumbai in 2000 and a whole new flavour of inadequacy. I joined an elite school where most children arrived in air-conditioned cars with drivers, while my sister and I, fresh from a small town in Gujarat, commuted on the local train. Our financial reality was not poor, but it didn't look rich in that setting.

To complete the humiliation starter pack, I was the tallest, most awkward girl in class. I was not quite 'girly' and definitely not a tomboy either— more like a confused giraffe trying to fit in at a flamingo party. The in-between-ness didn't earn me any cool points, just a steady diet of self-doubt and invisibility.

Meanwhile, my sister walked in as if it were her stage debut. She landed the lead in the school play, had teachers fawning over her, and made friends as though she were handing out sweets. I, on the other hand, hovered between average grades and full-blown stage fright. Beneath all that academic dread was a more sinister battle: My crumbling self-worth.

To keep up, I started pretending. I bragged about the latest arcade I had never visited, dropped imaginary holidays into conversations and pretended to know who Brad Pitt was.

In our new apartment complex, I became a different person. The shy, pretentious schoolgirl vanished, and in her place stood a bossy little dictator. I ran the gang of building children like it was a start-up. Cricket with a baseball bat? I scheduled it. Holi with water balloons? I managed distribution. Even my sister had to fall in line.

Outside, I reigned supreme. Inside, I was a cauldron of envy, shame, and insecurity. I wasn't particularly angry at her; I was furious at how invisible I felt next to her light. So, I did what hurt children do: I bullied her. What's more, I even recruited her to help me bully our house help's child.

His mother was a single parent who brought him to work, and it became our 'job' to keep him entertained. But we did not. We hung him upside down and made fun of him daily, as if he were a human stress ball we could toss around to feel better about ourselves. He didn't deserve any of it. He was a soft, gentle child. But that did not matter. He became our outlet because we did not know how to hold our own shame. And that's how it begins for most of us. When shame has nowhere to go, it becomes cruelty. What often looks like dominance is really just despair trying not to drown.

PERFORMANCE MODE: ON

After my bully era came puberty. The hormones hit, and so did the identity crisis. I was in an all-girls school, which meant the only men in my life were the neighbourhood building boys and the occasional glimpse of testosterone from an all-boys school we battled during interschool competitions. So, when MSN Messenger entered the chat, it was a dial-up doorway to dopamine.

Given my self-worth issues, I didn't feel desirable in real life. So, I did what any awkward thirteen-year-old drowning in insecurity would do: I became someone else. I created a fake MSN account and catfished unsuspecting boys by pretending to be my hot senior. I flirted, told elaborate stories, and performed confidence like it was a school play I never got cast in.

If you asked that version of me, hunched over a glowing screen, typing away like her life depended on it, what she wanted, she'd probably say: 'I want to matter. I want someone to choose me. I want to be wanted without having to pretend . . . but I'm scared the real me won't be enough.'

That fear didn't get left behind in the chatroom. It graduated with me.

By the time I hit my twenties, my shame had matured into performance art. When I moved back to Singapore in 2009 for college, I carried with me a superiority complex that had done a full pirouette. Now, I was 'too cool' to be Singaporean because I didn't speak Singlish. At the time, the government was literally running a 'Speak Good English' campaign, and I was convinced I was the campaign.

Add to that a 5'11 frame (in a country where the average height is fun-sized), sharp features, and a walk that screamed main character energy. I glided into MRT trains like a living perfume commercial. But in a class full of Singaporeans, I was a cultural outlier. The only other Singaporean I connected with was someone equally allergic to belonging. So, I found my people in the international student crowd.

Suddenly, my Indian identity, which once felt like baggage, became a badge. I hung out with Indians across faculties, talked Bollywood with unapologetic flair, and finally felt like I had a tribe. I also became a compulsive flirt, inserting myself into every conversation like coriander in Indian cooking—uninvited but always present.

Not surprisingly, I soon manifested a cute Indian boyfriend who was serving his National Service in the air force. All signs pointed to a smooth ride through Delululand.

But then came the plot twist: Sadhguru.

Within four years, my idea of love, identity, and reality itself got pulverised. I went from peacocking at parties to sobbing at the feet of a mystic. And for a moment, I genuinely considered renouncing it all for a lifetime of celibacy.

But the thing about spiritual portals is that they rarely lead where you expect. Just as I was fantasising about trading worldly pleasures for a bald head and an orange robe, the universe sent me a tempting little distraction in the form of an acceptance letter to the London Film School.

The matrix wasn't done with me yet.

London was a high-speed collision of dreams and delusions. Given my track record in school, the pressure to succeed in university sat on my chest like an ambitious elephant. Spirituality, which once anchored me, got shoved into a back drawer. Meditation? Who had time? I had deadlines, cigarettes, and overpriced cider to tend to. Instead of growing, I spiralled. In style, of course.

My spiritual journey didn't vanish. It got a glow-up in narcissistic packaging. I weaponised my new-found experience, using it to feel superior rather than sincere. I meditated loudly, distributed unsolicited advice like prasadam, and organised yoga classes for my whole class out of sheer spiritual performance.

I turned people into utility belts that served the purpose of stroking my ego. My 'friendships' were mostly functional. Even my generosity came with a subtle receipt.

I made myself indispensable on film sets, hoarded responsibilities, and micromanaged everything from lighting angles to other people's emotional reactions. My friendships were less 'let's connect' and more 'please validate my worthiness or kindly get out of the way'.

And while my sister partied it up in Singapore, squandering my parents' money like she was in a Bollywood bachelorette montage, I quietly judged her because I wasn't out at pubs every weekend. I was better. Or so I told myself. Looking back, my restraint wasn't selflessness. It was strategic superiority. A subtle, smug way to tell myself I mattered more because I suffered silently and sacrificed with flair.

I had built an empire of control, performance, and pretence. And just when I thought I was safe inside it, admired, adored, and untouchable, the universe threw in a wildcard: Ziad.

Spiritual Firewall

I met Ziad through a casual Isha community outing to Camden Lock. He was a former Lebanese journalist turned full-time artist. He was creative, intense, funny, and someone who, unlike me, had actually done a lot of the spiritual work. Not just the 'read a book and quote Osho on dates' kind, but the sit-in-the-fire-of-your-own-shadows kind.

Our first date ended with a kiss that felt like a thousand truths crashing into one moment. I remember thinking, 'Uh oh! Here goes my peace.'

And then came another cosmic joke: Ziad was the same age as my father. Literally. Their birthdays were a week apart. He was recently divorced, with a daughter slightly younger than me. To add to it, he was a Taurus—just like my dad and the love of my life who had shattered my heart before I arrived in London. The universe wasn't just sending me signs; it was throwing flashcards in my face labelled 'Daddy Issues 101'.

But I didn't run. I leaned in even though it was inconvenient, because it felt real, authentic, and genuine. That was something I hadn't known in a while. Ziad saw parts of me I had buried.

He met my pain with presence, my chaos with calm, my insecurities with tenderness. And yet, I couldn't relax. I was busy managing the optics of our connection and curating my shame like an art exhibit.

When my sister came to visit, I introduced them. Because clearly, what's spiritual growth without a dose of masochism? Her reaction was exactly what I feared: Subtle judgement, silent disapproval, and that look only a sister can give. The one that says, 'Really?' without saying a word.

That's when the spiral began. Not because Ziad did anything wrong, but because I was still operating out of shame about our age gap and performing acceptance. I turned his vulnerability into a checklist. Every emotional confession from him became a problem to fix. Every shadow he shared became a mirror I didn't want to look into. I thought I was helping him heal, but really, I was trying to heal myself through him.

And then life did what it does when you're ignoring your truth: It threw a plot twist.

The night before he left London for good to move to Beirut, we made love. It was tender and real. Days later, I found out I was pregnant.

When I told him over the phone, his response was honest but blunt: 'Well, you know what to do.' I knew he wasn't being callous; he was just being practical. But shame has selective hearing. I didn't hear practicality—I heard rejection and translated it into abandonment. My inner victim lit up like a Christmas tree, and I projected every ounce of my buried pain onto him. I made him the villain in a story that was never his to begin with.

The timing of this plot twist was such that I was caught between a bank account with insufficient funds and trying to direct my term film. Asking my parents for more money meant having to share the truth with them. What would I tell them? That I was pregnant by a man their age? Not even the best screenplay could make that ending work.

Guru Purnima was around the corner, and for the first time in years, I sat down to meditate—like really meditate to surrender, not just show off. That night, I gave everything to the unknown—all my shame, confusion, and fear.

And then magically, something shifted. I miscarried the very next day. There was no pain, no hospital drama—just a strange stillness, like the universe had intervened and said, 'Welcome back on track.' That should have been my cue to stop my performative spirituality and actually embrace it. But my problem was solved, so I went back to my old ways.

The shame surrounding Ziad and this entire incident lingered. For over a decade, I buried that story like it didn't exist. I never told my parents. So much so that I didn't even include it in the first draft of this book. And then, the final twist arrived.

Soon after I had completed the first draft, I got a message from Ziad's daughter telling me that he had died two days before my birthday. He had suffered a sudden heart attack, and he was gone.

I froze for a minute before I burst out laughing at the design of the universe. I had unfinished business, and the story I thought I had tucked away came roaring back, louder than ever. How dare I not tell it!

In the days that followed, I scrolled through old e-mails from 2013 and found one he had sent me shortly after the miscarriage. He had poured his heart out, apologising for not being there, expressing his care. I never read it or replied because I was too consumed with my own story to care about his. That e-mail hit me like a punch I didn't see coming.

The thing about buried stories is that they don't stay buried. They live in your body, your reactions, and your relationships. They wait patiently for the next trigger to pull them back up. Ziad's passing ripped the bandage off a decade of suppressed emotion, revealing just how deeply programmed I still was.

Ziad's story didn't end here, but for now, I will press the pause button. Because before we can even begin to talk about death and liberation, we need to understand what's actually driving us: The deeply wired, often invisible responses we've inherited from a lifetime of fear, guilt, and shame. The survival scripts we mistake for personality and the knee-jerk patterns we call 'just the way I am.'

Human_Behaviour.exe

There was a time I thought 'that's just the way I am' was a statement of authenticity. It felt bold and empowering, as though I was standing up for my truth. But over the years, I've realised that sentence is less about self-acceptance and more about giving our inner chaos a free pass.

Let's get one thing straight: Nobody is *just* the way they are. Not me, not you, not that ex who thinks ghosting is a personality trait. We're all patchworks of inherited patterns, ancestral coping strategies, and emotional defence systems dressed up as quirks. And the biggest lie we've internalised is that these behaviours are fixed, hardwired, or worse, that they *are* us.

The truth is that most of it is simply software we downloaded without ever reading the terms and conditions.

In the beginning, life was relatively simple. Our ancestors wandered in small tribes, sharing firewood and gossip, defending one another from the occasional tiger attack. There was no 'inner child healing' back then, just surviving the outer wilderness. You weren't fretting over your self-worth if your worth literally depended on spotting a snake in the grass before it spotted you.

Then came clothes and civilisation, and everything went sideways.

Suddenly, there were boundaries, fences, borders, and ownership. Insecurity was promoted from a quirk to a full-blown institution. Fights over food expanded into fights over land and resources. Scarcity bred fear, and fear gave birth to shame.

From that point onwards, history became a high-stakes drama of dominance. The Peloponnesian War was basically an ancient sibling rivalry between Athens and Sparta. Then came Rome, which built more walls than your average emotionally unavailable ex.

Even modern nations act like insecure teenagers at prom. The Cold War wasn't a battle of ideologies; it was an elaborate pissing contest between two superpowers hoarding nuclear weapons like Pokémon cards, terrified of looking weak. It was essentially a global, passive-aggressive 'DON'T MESS WITH ME' text in all caps.

Fast forward to today, and the UN resembles a high-school cafeteria. Nations nervously eye one another, gossip, form cliques, and guard their lunch tables (read: borders), while pretending it's all about diplomacy. Racism, sexism, and economic inequality all have their roots in shame and fear. Toddlers scream 'Mine!' over toys; adults do the same with land, resources, and power. We just gave it fancier names.

Look closer and you'll see the same mess in your own dynamics. We hoard affection like Cold War missiles. We build walls when we feel vulnerable. Because somewhere, someone told us that needing love was weak. And we believed them.

Sibling rivalry is really just the toddler version. Competing for validation, attention, and that sacred title of 'Who did Mum love more?' And no, it doesn't end in childhood. It grows up, buys property, and starts comparing credit scores.

Even love, our most sacred institution, is infiltrated. To love someone fully is to reveal the scared, messy, unfiltered parts of yourself. And we'd rather die than do that. So, we use marriage to escape the real void: *If I lock this down, maybe I'll finally feel safe.* Cue the big-fat-Indian-wedding, the awkward photoshoots, and the lifelong subscription to performative partnership—all to prove to the world: 'Look, I'm worthy enough to have someone who will tolerate me for life.'

Insecurity doesn't stop with how we see ourselves; it insists on warping how we see other people, too. Judging others becomes a sport, a twisted kind of mental CrossFit where we're constantly comparing ourselves to everyone around us. *At least I'm not as messy as that guy,* or *she's not even that smart.* It's the adult version of 'I'm better than you', except instead of playground bragging rights, we do it through passive-aggressive comments, or painfully curated social media posts.

The worst part? It doesn't even work. Tearing others down to build ourselves up is like trying to fix a broken mirror by punching it harder. We get a fleeting sense of superiority by breaking others, but it only isolates us further. The more we compare, the less we connect. The more we perform, the less we relate. Eventually, it's just us, stuck in a competition no one asked to join, clutching our invisible trophies of 'at least I'm not them'.

And this isn't only personal, it's planetary. Every war is a grotesque mirror reflecting humanity's unresolved emotional chaos. Every conflict or political spectacle is just a projection of our collective inner war with shame, fear, and insecurity. The same impulses that make you want to make your ex suffer are the ones that make world leaders build walls and launch missiles.

Because war, like ghosting, is often a reaction, not a resolution.

But here's the light at the end of this emotionally exhausting tunnel: None of this is our fault. It's just code. Programming. A complex system of cultural conditioning and emotional muscle memory that finds expression through subconscious scripts.

SUBCONSCIOUS_SCRIPT.BAT

If you're not familiar with it, let me introduce you to the command system that runs 98 per cent of human interaction. It's the part of you that flinches when someone says, 'We need to talk,' or turns your partner's silence into a true-crime plot. It's the inner algorithm that decides:

- If I feel scared, I'll get angry
- If I feel guilty, I'll blame you
- If I feel ashamed, I'll go cold and distant
- If I feel not-enough, I'll pretend to be more-than

We like to call it a reaction. But let's be honest: It's just emotional autopilot gone rogue.

Every time someone doesn't text back, every time we're left on read, every time a tone feels vaguely condescending—boom! Programme activated. Before we even blink, the body has launched into fight, flight, freeze, or fawn; already rehearsing a shower monologue and drafting closing arguments.

Why? Because somewhere along the way, we absorbed a dangerous idea: *You are not enough unless you prove otherwise.* And so we perform. With productivity. With perfectionism. With justifications, fake kindness, edited selfies, and painstakingly curated humility.

At the root of it all is fear—specifically, the fear of being exposed as 'not special'. The possibility that we're just ordinary, wounded humans with unhealed baggage is intolerable to the ego.

So, we run internal PR campaigns, marketing ourselves to ourselves. We twist reality into a version we can bear: One where we're always a little wiser, kinder, or more aware than those around us.

Shame whispers: 'Hide. Avoid. Control how others see you at all costs'. So, we ghost, dodge hard conversations, and skip social events where we might get exposed as flawed. We enter emotional witness protection, hiding from the truth of our own mess.

Ironically, the more we hide, the tighter shame grips. We become master architects of façades. On the surface: Yoga routines, meditation retreats, soul-aligned journalling. Behind the scenes: Emotional clutter and a laundry pile taller than our inner child's unmet needs. The gap between performance and reality widens until the performance becomes reality.

And when that illusion is threatened, manipulation kicks in. We gaslight, guilt-trip, or future-fake. Not because we're bad people, but because we're terrified of being seen as messy and human.

Future-faking is the ego's favourite trick: 'I'll be better tomorrow.' We dangle hope before others and ourselves. It isn't deception; we believe it. Because facing the present would mean confronting discomfort. And we've been taught that discomfort is dangerous, that not being okay is a failing rather than a fact of life.

When all else fails, we reach for the victim card: 'Life has wronged me. Others let me down. My childhood was unfair.' This narrative demands no change—just sympathy. And in a world allergic to accountability, it often works.

But numbing is the real MVP. Alcohol, food, sex, shopping, scrolling—we use them to soften the sharp edges of self-awareness. Because simply sitting silently brings us face to face with the one truth we resist: No amount of sex, spending, or spirulina smoothies can save us from ourselves.

The problem isn't that we do these things; it's that we defend them. We treat our survival responses as sacred, and gaslight anyone who questions them: 'Oh! It's just for fun. That's not what I meant. You're making things up.'

Beneath all of this is one fear: Change. Because real change requires dismantling the entire illusion we've built. The great irony? The very defences we use to protect ourselves are the ones that destroy intimacy.

Take perfectionism. We strive to be perfect sons, daughters, partners, and employees. But perfectionism is simply the gold-medal mask of shame. It isn't about excellence; it's about terror. Every task becomes a performance. Every conversation, a tightrope walk over the abyss of 'What if I disappoint them?'

And when perfectionism fails, we activate Plan B: The Saviour Complex. If I can't be flawless, I'll be indispensable. We play therapist, fixer, Mother Teresa—sacrificing joy to outrun invisibility.

Add to this mix a generous helping of comparison, judgement, overthinking, and numbing, and what you've got isn't a personality. It's a trauma-management system. Identity reduced to reaction.

Here is the liberating truth: Your reactions are not your prison. You can edit them into conscious responses. You are not 'just the way you are'. You are the choices you made when you were five and frightened, twelve and shamed, twenty-five and rejected.

And now? You're old enough to choose again.

Identity_Crash.log

If we are not our shame, guilt, fears, or insecurities, then who are we?

This is the million-dollar question that's puzzled everyone from ancient sages to your friend who is addicted to Ayahuasca and calls himself a Shaman. We say 'I' constantly, but what does it mean? Is it the job you hustle to keep, the flat you just redecorated, the body you drag to the gym?

Let us start simple. We don't say 'I am a body'. We say I have a body, as if it's a leased car. My eyes, my hands, my thighs—as though they could be swapped at a cosmic repair shop. This linguistic glitch hides a deeper truth: If you *have* a body, who's the one doing the having?

The ego would love you to think it is the one. It is obsessed with appearance and status, panicking at wrinkles or follower drops. It ties worth to the exterior as if survival depends on it. But hair greys, waistlines shift, limbs are lost—and yet *you* remain. The body is packaging: Functional, sometimes fabulous, but not the essence.

Then there are thoughts. Descartes said, 'I think, therefore I am.' More like, *I overthink, therefore I have anxiety*! Thoughts are uninvited party guests. Believing you *are* your thoughts is like mistaking every guest for the host; never mind half of them are conspiracy theorists or drunk uncles.

Emotions are like the weather. One moment sunny, the next you're crying in an Uber. The ego turns passing moods into fixed identity: Rejected means unlovable; success means god-like status. But the real you is not the cloud cover. You're the sky behind it.

In *Midnight's Children,* Salman Rushdie wrote, 'I am the sum total of everything that went before me.' Beautiful, poetic, and partly true. Yes, the past shapes you. But it doesn't define you. That's the ego's mixtape: Scars and stories stitched into an illusion of separateness. This is me, it insists, parading credentials, traumas, and photos like a slideshow at group therapy.

But you are not your slideshow.

The ego builds identity out of your CV, your relationships, and your skincare routine. It whispers: *You are your status, your failures, your achievements.* And because it's loud, we believe it.

This illusion exhausts us. We chase applause, love, validation—anything to feel temporarily complete. We curate a self that's acceptable to others and forget how to simply *be.*

Now, don't get it twisted; the ego has uses. It sets boundaries, makes appointments, and stops you from drunk-dialling your ex at 3 a.m. But when it runs the show, life becomes an endless audition for worthiness.

Fear of failure, rejection, loss, and death—it's all the ego clinging to control. But here's the joke: The thing we cling to isn't real. It's like sawing the branch you sit on while panicking about the fall. The branch was never real.

Stop playing the ego's game, and something wild happens: Peace. Not dull peace, but the kind that comes when you no longer chase or defend anything. The kind that knows: *I don't need to prove I exist. I am.*

The yogic insight of Shiva as 'No-thing' or 'That Which Is Not' isn't a poetic flourish. It points to the essence of self, beyond body, identity, and emotion. Shiva represents what remains when all that is *not you* falls away.

To embody Shiva is to witness. To stop clinging to your drama and watch it like a rerun you already know by heart. Not cold detachment, but freedom—the realisation that your worth isn't up for debate.

The 'I' you have been seeking is not in a job title, a soulmate, or a personal brand. It's the one that's been quietly watching all along. Not performing. Not posturing. Simply aware.

That's not nothing. That's everything.

Manual Override

Deconditioning is a messy business. It is like peeling an onion. Layer by layer, you strip away everything society, family, and culture have dumped on you. And just when you think you've reached the core, there's another layer waiting to make you cry.

We spend years assembling an identity from other people's expectations: Be the good child, the loyal friend, the hard worker, the one who never disappoints. Then one day, something cracks—heartbreak, burnout, or the gnawing sense that your life has been one long performance review. And suddenly the question drops: '*Wait . . . is any of this me?*'

This is where the journey begins. You start to unlearn programmed responses and figure out what's truly you and what's just societal fluff. Speaking your truth in this world is like walking into a battlefield armed with a water balloon. The moment you choose authenticity, you become a target for projections, judgements, and unsolicited advice from people who'd rather you stay comfortably fake.

Your honesty unsettles others because it reflects their own unacknowledged truths. So they lash out. You'll be called too emotional, too intense, too immature. They'll twist your words and weaponise your openness, making your growth feel like betrayal. But the only thing more exhausting than being real is pretending to be someone you're not.

Take relationships. You show up honest, clear, emotionally available, and tell them you want them. No games, no manipulation. And what happens? They run or call you 'too much'. Then they chase someone who holds back, mistake that for mystery, and months later wonder why they feel unfulfilled. We reject truth in others because we haven't made peace with it in ourselves.

Family is similar. You finally tell your parents that their constant nagging about your career choices is driving you insane, and suddenly you're 'ungrateful'.

'We sacrificed so much for you!' they protest, as if reminding you of tuition fees cancels out your truth.

And the workplace? Speak up in a meeting, question a policy, suggest a new approach—and bam! You're the 'difficult' one. Colleagues tiptoe, managers tighten reins, and you wonder if you should have just nodded along, faking enthusiasm. Companies plaster words like innovation and authenticity on their walls, but God forbid you actually practise them.

Even the spiritual world isn't immune. You're told to be compassionate, forgiving, humble, and selfless. Wonderful ideals—until they clash with your truth. 'Transcend anger,' they say. But what if your authentic self needs to scream, or even hit someone first? Spiritual bypassing is real. We're shamed for not fitting the peaceful yogi archetype, when healing often begins with honouring the messy, primal parts we've been conditioned to disown.

The unglamorous truth: Authenticity isn't emotional striptease or chronic oversharing. It's not parading your inner child around like a chandelier. The more anchored you are in who you truly are, the less you need to announce it.

Realness doesn't always come with a megaphone. Sometimes it arrives as a pause, a half-smile, a well-placed silence. Restraint isn't repression; it's refinement.

When unconscious, we wore masks out of fear—desperate to be liked, safe, acceptable. Once conscious, the mask becomes optional, even useful. Not as a lie, but as a filter: Not everything true needs to be spoken, and not everyone deserves a front-row seat to your soul.

When authenticity matures past its rebellious phase, it becomes selective. It knows when to disrupt and when to withdraw. When to reveal and when to remain enigmatic. It isn't about being understood by everyone; it's about being at peace even when you're not. Most importantly, it ceases to be a raw outburst and becomes a quiet power that doesn't confuse vulnerability with leakage.

The more you live from this space, the clearer it becomes: Authenticity is not the destination of the spiritual path but the doorway. Before peace comes truth. Before enlightenment, excavation. Before you become light, you must pass through the raw, muddy terrain of what it means to be real.

System Reset

Naga doesn't just mean 'snake'; it also means 'naked'. And Shiva? He didn't just wear a snake; he was naked in the truest sense. While other gods adorned themselves in gold and silk, Shiva appeared in cremation grounds, smeared in ash—a disruptive rebellion against the polished façades of the world.

Then there are the *Naga Sadhus*, Shiva's die-hard fan club. These fierce ascetics didn't merely follow his teachings; they became the teachings. Roaming the edges of society, indifferent to rules, norms, or deodorant, they stripped themselves of all that was false—physically, mentally, emotionally, and spiritually. Their nakedness was essentially a return to the Garden of Eden.

The Naga Sadhus know something most of us don't: Shame only survives in shadows. It thrives on secrecy, pretence, and curated reputations. Shiva's way? Burn it all. The moment you bring it into the light, own it, laugh at it, and dance with it, it crumbles. Once exposed, there's nothing left for the world to exploit—no image to protect, no illusion to uphold. Just you, raw, radiant, real.

Not everyone can handle that kind of naked truth. Certainly not Daksha, Shiva's father-in-law and CEO of the status quo. If Shiva was the wild mountain breeze, Daksha was the office cubicle personified: Orderly, proper, and obsessed with appearances. When his daughter, Sati, married this ash-smeared enigma who meditated through eclipses, Daksha was mortified.

Determined to restore 'dignity', Daksha threw the biggest Yagna in celestial history—a VVIP-only fire ritual so lavish even the gods had to RSVP. Guess who wasn't on the guest list? Shiva.

Sati, heartbroken but hopeful, went anyway, perhaps believing love could melt pride. But she walked into a furnace of humiliation. Daksha belittled her beloved in front of gods, sages, and a thousand watchful eyes, mocking Shiva's wildness, lack of decorum, and refusal to fit into boxes. In that ritual fire, something broke.

Consumed by the shame Daksha hurled and the pain of seeing her love disrespected, Sati walked into the sacred fire and let it all burn—her body, her role as a daughter, her need for approval. That fire wasn't suicide; it was purification.

When Shiva learnt of her death, he created and sent Veerabhadra, who stormed Daksha's perfect gathering and, literally, took his head off. But Shiva's wrath wasn't born of grief or vengeance. It was a cosmic correction. Because then, in a move only Shiva could make, he forgave Daksha and revived him—but not as he was. He gave him the head of a goat—humble and earthy.

Sati didn't vanish into myth; she reincarnated as Parvati. Same soul, upgraded code. She didn't return seeking validation. She returned whole. She became Shiva's Shakti. Having walked through fire, on the other side of shame, she found sovereignty.

This isn't just mythology; it's shadow work.

Every time life roasts us in the flames of embarrassment, rejection, or ego-death, we're invited into our own yagna. Let the lies burn. Shed the layers never ours to carry. Stop proving, start being. Humiliation isn't the end. It's the beginning. The ego gets grilled, but the soul emerges golden.

Shiva teaches us that destruction is mercy in disguise. It clears the noise, topples falsehoods, and makes space for truth. You don't need rebirth in another life—you can be reborn now: every time you choose truth over image, let go instead of holding on, stop hiding and let yourself be seen, even if it means standing naked in a world addicted to costumes.

System Reset isn't about erasing who you are. It's about stripping away who you never were.

SOLULU 4

Be Shamelessly Real

'You either die a hero or live long enough to see yourself become the villain.' If you've ever dared to speak your truth, you'll know what this means. Authenticity requires courage, and courage invites discomfort. People may abuse you, ghost you, project their insecurities, and try to cast you as 'crazy' or 'sick'. You become a mirror reflecting what they've avoided in themselves, and they'll do everything to break that mirror.

Yet authenticity is life's greatest filter. It clears out those never meant to walk with you and makes space for those who align with your highest vibration—those who can hold space for your truth without running for the hills. Speaking your truth is about letting go of the fake and making room for what's real.

Those who have broken free from the mould of 'What will people think?' will attest that it feels like a breath of fresh air. Yet many areas of life still operate under the fear of perception. We lie, cheat, gossip, compete, and exclude to feed the ego's hunger for a mirage of perfection. None of us are flawless; all of us are a little unhinged. Our mission? Uncover the turmoil, diagnose it, and heal it.

Start by ditching the need for approval, validation, or attention. Make peace with mistakes, faults, insecurities, and uncertainties—they're part of being human. It's okay to be disliked, judged as arrogant, or even perceived as incompetent. It is okay to be the villain in someone else's story—or even your own. It is more than okay to be cringe. The important thing is to be truthful to yourself.

Weave honesty and authenticity into your daily life, beginning at home—the most sacred space for growth. At work, when faced with impossible deadlines—speak your truth instead of spinning tales or excuses. The right people, opportunities, and experiences will gravitate to you when you act with integrity.

Even in the curated world of social media, sharing your truth—your struggles, fears, messy thoughts—may feel exposing. Yet beneath glossy highlight reels, everyone is just as lost. Vulnerability invites real connection and reminds us we're in this together.

Through trial and error, you'll learn responsible authenticity. True authenticity isn't oversharing or dumping unprocessed emotions. It's discernment: Knowing when to roar your truth from the rooftops and when to hold it close, recognising that not everyone is ready for front-row seats to your life.

Delulu 5
LOVE IS BLIND

'It is only with the heart that one can see rightly; what is essential is invisible to the eye.'

– Antoine de Saint-Exupéry

THE LOVE DRUG

We enter this world with the grace of a drunk karaoke singer, screaming, demanding, desperate to be held. A chest to rest on, a drop of milk, a little eye contact—and we're pacified. Our needs are laughably basic at the start. But don't be fooled! Behind that gummy smile lies a nascent Machiavellian genius.

By three months old, most babies have already discovered that fake crying is far more effective. Welcome to our first crash course in emotional manipulation. From then on, we learn that love isn't free; it must be earned, bargained for, sometimes theatrically extorted.

Fast-forward to adulthood, and nothing's really changed. The props just got fancier. We sulk, withdraw, overachieve, pose, flirt, filter, and thirst-trap—all in the same relentless pursuit: To be seen, adored, to matter. We just swap the wail for a CV, the crib for a corner office, and the blankie for a Birkin.

Strip it all down, and every pursuit—sex, relationships, marriage, money, possessions, fame, knowledge, wisdom, abs—is a dialect of the same prayer: *Please love me.* Some whisper it, some demand it, but everyone is chanting.

And when love doesn't come the way we imagined, we fall apart. Some of us crumble quietly; others get performative with revenge bodies, better selfies, or well-timed passive-aggressive status updates. The world's greatest tragedies, pettiest feuds, and most dramatic break-up texts all stem from the same place: Someone didn't feel loved enough.

We like to pretend we're rational, but let someone make our stomach flutter and suddenly we're emotional raccoons, pawing through the trash for scraps of validation. Neurochemistry doesn't help. Dopamine convinces us we've found 'the one' after we've known them for all of eight minutes. Serotonin keeps us checking our phones like slot machines. Oxytocin has us leaving toothbrushes after date two. And cortisol drags us through heartbreak like a medieval torturer.

We are not like addicts. We *are* addicts. Love is the original high; heartbreak, the cold-turkey crash that sends us spiralling into bad haircuts. But unlike other drugs, love can't be bought, timed, or tricked. It arrives when it pleases, lingers if it wants, and vanishes without apology. The tighter we grip, the quicker it slips. And yet every myth, scripture, war, wedding, pop song, and therapy session spins around its axis.

But why? Why this endless obsession? Why does every human crave it, fight for it, write about it, die for it?

Because beneath the wreckage of failed crushes and toxic entanglements, something in us whispers that love is not just a feeling—it's a doorway. A passage older than time and bigger than biology. Why else would every culture, from cave paintings to K-pop, mark the heart as its throne? Why not the brain? Or the liver, which frankly does more heavy lifting?

It is because, deep down, we know that the *Anahata*—the Heart Chakra—is the energetic centre of love. Not in some airy-fairy, incense-burning, 'let's all hold hands' kind of way, but in a very real, physiological, and metaphysical sense. The heart space is where we process connection, where we feel the pull towards something beyond ourselves.

This addiction to love isn't random. What we think is a mess of failed crushes, toxic relationships, and awkward situationships is actually a curriculum. Each heartbreak, each infatuation, each inexplicable longing is a chapter in a divine education.

The trouble begins when we misunderstand love as a transaction. When we try to earn it, manipulate it, and keep it—that's when we end up going in circles.

CUPID'S ARROW

My first boyfriend in Singapore was the kind of 'Good Indian Boy' you could bring home without anyone breaking out in hives. At the time, that suited me fine. I had just finished Inner Engineering with Sadhguru, was acing my classes, and life looked like a neatly balanced Excel sheet. I thought love was supposed to be like that—tidy, controlled, polite.

Then came the summer of 2011. I flew back to Mumbai. Weighed down by the overachiever guilt of not doing enough, I volunteered to film a three-week drama workshop at the National Centre for

Performing Arts. My sister was interning there, too, and I figured some harmless B-roll would keep me busy. The universe, of course, had other plans.

Day one of the workshop happened to coincide with the birthday of one of the instructors: Sankar. Even his name—another form of Shiva—was cosmic foreshadowing I was too dense to notice. I first saw him leading an exercise where participants held a torturous posture while he chanted the *Shiva Tandava Stotram*, a chant I was familiar with.

He had a lean frame draped in a Jinbei, a Brahmin tuft of hair, and hazel eyes that seemed to pierce through your soul. Women swarmed around him, only to retreat when they discovered he was married. To me, though, he was background noise. I wasn't impressed. Not even curious.

Apparently, that made me stand out. Mid-class, he stopped, looked straight at me, and announced, 'I'm known to kick photographers out. I'm surprised I'm letting you walk around like this.'

I froze, half-expecting to be tossed out, but then he smirked, like my lack of awe had qualified me for some invisible game.

A few days later, during lunch, we finally spoke. When I mentioned I studied in Singapore, his eyes lit up. 'I studied there, too,' he said, before breaking into a perfect imitation of the MRT announcement in all four languages—intonation, robotic pauses, the whole performance. Up until then, he'd carried himself like a man who ate the Vedas for breakfast. Suddenly, he was a stand-up comic. For the first time, I saw him.

Life, never one to miss a punchline, added slapstick. A casual family movie night the same week ended with me slipping on the stairs, slamming my head against a wall, and fainting—complete with cerebrospinal fluid leaking from my ear.

I woke up in a hospital bed with a minor concussion. My sister scrolled her phone nonchalantly. 'By the way,' she said, 'Sankar wants to visit you.'

'Why?' I croaked.

'I don't know. He's weird. I told him you'll be back to work soon.'

Later that night, my phone buzzed with a message: 'Sending you healing Chi.' At the time, I didn't realise this was the first domino in a fourteen-year saga.

When I returned to the workshop, something felt . . . altered. Maybe it was the concussion. Or maybe slamming my crown chakra into a wall had unlocked a portal no one had warned me about.

One afternoon during a t'ai chi class, he asked me to put the camera down and join. I hesitated; he insisted. When he adjusted my posture—deliberately, playfully—my whole nervous system lit up like a Christmas tree. The air between us crackled with something neither of us dared to name.

A few days later came the wrap party. People mingled, swapped numbers, clung to the last scraps of connection. He walked up and kissed me—not on the cheek, but a slow, deliberate kiss on the forehead—then walked off to smoke a cigarette. The whole table fell silent. I got up and followed him outside.

That night, we sat outside Mumbai's famous Leopold Café, talking for hours about everything and nothing. At some point, he realised he'd lost his wife's camera, but what he worried about more was how to spend his last day in Mumbai before his train to Kerala.

By morning, we were at an IMAX screening of *Kung Fu Panda*. Watching a lost panda search for inner peace—also no coincidence. I even invited his co-instructor to keep it from looking like a date. But the way he bought me ice cream during the interval was full rom-com energy, the kind that says, 'I'm pretending this isn't a date, but here's your Häagen-Dazs, my lady.'

When he was leaving Mumbai, he handed me a book on yogic techniques. I thought it was a nerdy gift; in hindsight, it was an initiation, a manual my soul had signed up for but my brain hadn't caught up with. We parted with a long, deliberate hug, and as the lift doors closed behind him, I felt an invisible thread tighten across my chest, knotted at both ends.

The next day, I realised my sunglasses were missing. Hours later, a photo arrived: Sankar wearing them. Caption: 'I'll return them when you visit South India.'

I should've known he wasn't flirting. That was the first breadcrumb.

Because I was visiting South India. I'd told him the night of the wrap party that I was heading to the Isha Yoga Center the following week. By some divine set-up, he not only lived 60 km away but also owned some land in a forest just over the mountain from the yoga centre.

'Let's camp there,' he suggested casually.

And just like that, the universe pulled out its drumsticks and went *ba-dum-tss*.

Those Three Words

Something about the thread between us begged to be tested, so I tossed another card into the deck. I invited Sankar to join me for a full moon ritual at the newly opened Devi Temple at Isha. One suggestion spiralled into another, and before we knew it, a five-day itinerary had planned itself.

When he arrived at Isha on a full moon night, the air crackled.

Sankar was every bit the Brahmin: Sacred thread across his chest, mantras at the ready, and just the right amount of smugness about his ritual know-how. He also had several bones to pick with Sadhguru and Isha, but beneath the surface grumbling, he understood the essence. Besides, the fact that he had made the effort to meet me there meant more than the commentary.

Despite having separate rooms, we ended up talking for hours in his. Just as the silence thickened, he smirked and said, 'Don't be too shocked if you wake up to find me without my mundu.' For context, a mundu is essentially a South Indian man-skirt—the final barrier between culture and chaos. By morning, mercifully, the mundu was still guarding the gates.

The next day, we crossed the mountain to his land near Malleswaran Peak, pitched a tent in the monsoon forest, and let the rain hammer a rhythm section above us. Candles flickered, chips went soggy, cigarettes burned half-finished, and the sexual tension between us was enough to power the national grid.

Then, in the middle of philosophy and silence, I farted. Not a discreet little whisper—an unapologetic brass section. He wrinkled his nose. 'Ew. In all these years, my wife has never farted in front of me.' I blinked, caught between pity for his marriage and awe at her digestive discipline. We both collapsed into laughter, because really, what else could we do?

Time bent oddly in that tent. Eyes lingered, hands brushed, breath slowed. One small peck landed. Just one. He was married. I was in a relationship. Neither of us had planned betrayal, but something larger than both of us had clearly RSVP'd.

Eventually, we drifted to sleep in each other's arms—not lovers, not friends, just two souls that had no language to name what they'd just discovered.

The morning was strangely ordinary. No shame, no awkwardness. We packed up the tent like it was any other damp camping trip. He dropped me in Thrissur before heading off for work, but when I woke the next day, he was there again—sitting quietly by my bed, not in a creepy way, but like he was still puzzling over what had happened.

With one night left before I was due to leave, he suggested Kochi. We checked into a creaky old hotel, high ceilings and one king-sized bed. Neither of us crossed the invisible line. We lay on opposite sides, breathing into the fog of unspoken feelings.

The next morning, he drove me to the airport. I flew back to Mumbai, but the thread between us only became tighter. Messages turned constant—confessions, philosophies, jokes, and dreams.

A week later, on a flight back to Singapore, I couldn't hold it in anymore. I typed out everything—raw, messy, unguarded—and hit send. Seconds before take-off, his reply blinked onto my screen:

'I love you.'

Three words, launched into the sky as the plane lifted off the ground. It felt like the start of something enormous.

And, God help me, I didn't know then just how enormous it would be.

Chasing Butterflies

Sexual attraction confused me for most of my adult life. Not because I didn't feel it, but because I couldn't decode the rules. Who turned it on? Who controlled the switch? Why are we magnetised to some people while others—often objectively more attractive—barely register a blip? I knew the textbook theories: Pheromones, symmetry, and evolutionary biology. But they never explained *me*. I could stand across from the most aesthetically perfect man, admire him like art in a gallery, and feel absolutely nothing. My brain would applaud politely, but my body would be asleep.

Then came Sankar.

From the moment we parted ways after that first meeting, I couldn't stop thinking about him. It was visceral, feral—like my body had quietly installed a compass, and he was true north. And he didn't exactly make it easier. His messages came often, laced with warmth and intent, making it clear he felt the same pull.

Trying to be a responsible partner, I confessed to my boyfriend in Singapore. I told him I couldn't stay present, that my mind kept drifting back to Sankar. It wasn't noble, but it was honest.

To his credit, he stayed calm. He reminded me that Sankar was married, that this path led nowhere, and that I deserved better. He wasn't wrong. So, I tried to be 'good'. I cut Sankar off, told him to focus on his marriage. Blocked him. Unblocked him. Blocked him again. The pull was relentless—silent, invisible, impossible to ignore.

My boyfriend also knew that the only spiritual teacher I truly listened to was Sadhguru, and he began using that knowledge to control me. Over time, the calm exterior gave way to someone watchful, manipulative, and almost obsessive. Nine months later, when I learnt the extremes to which he had gone to control me, whatever tenderness I'd felt vanished. I ended it—and ran straight into Sankar's arms.

That summer, on his thirty-third birthday, I flew to Pondicherry. With its French façades and salt-heavy air, the city already felt like a film set waiting for a love story. For a year, we had convinced ourselves this was wrong. But when we finally crossed that line, it didn't feel wrong at all.

Our first union wasn't reckless or frantic. It was deliberate, reverent—like replaying an ancient memory frame by frame. Every moment felt orchestrated by the stars. It wasn't lust that drew me in; it was sacred recognition.

I assumed he felt it, too, because from that night onwards, we couldn't stop. Every evening at 11:00 p.m., my phone lit up. We spoke across time zones, across roles, across reason. The obsession deepened.

Soon, my so-called spiritual journey became an elaborate travel plan to see him again. Sankar was the hidden footnote behind every programme I signed up for: *Bhava Spandana*, *Shoonya*, *Yogasanas*. The only one I skipped was *Samyama*—the final boss. Each time I walked out of a retreat, there he was, waiting like a divine chauffeur, ready to spirit me away for stolen days.

It's strange—I barely remember my first experiences of intimacy in earlier relationships. I know they happened, but my body must have been in airplane mode. With Sankar, I remembered everything.

However, here's the part I never admitted for over a decade: Sankar taught me, without ever saying it aloud, that sexuality could be a form of currency. A suggestive message, a photograph, a word of longing—and suddenly he was present, tender, attentive. I began to mistake desire for devotion, attention for love. My body became the offering; his approval, the altar. Somewhere in that exchange, I lost myself completely.

No one tells you what happens when your worth becomes tethered to how much someone else wants you. Desire starts to feel like oxygen. You don't flirt for fun—you flirt because it's the only language you know for visibility. Even after him, I carried that pattern. If I could make someone desire me, I believed I mattered.

Twisted? Certainly. But also transformative. Because in the wreckage of that entanglement, I finally saw the truth: Attraction was never really about the other person. It was always a mirror. The butterflies I thought I was chasing were only ever trying to lead me home—to myself.

The G(od) Spot

The amount we do in the name of sex is straight up ridiculous. We sculpt abs, swipe right, write mediocre poetry, light overpriced candles, survive awkward foreplay, and squeeze into lingerie that turns into dental floss mid-action—all in pursuit of one slippery, ten-second fireworks display.

Sex is capitalism's crown jewel. It sells perfume, protein shakes, pillows, and practically anything you can Photoshop onto a half-naked body. Evolution calls it survival. Freud blamed your mother. Porn markets it as a full-time lifestyle. But beneath the hormones and algorithms lies a less-advertised truth: Sexual energy is rocket fuel for awakening.

Sex is, in fact, one of our first spiritual teachers—not the act itself, but the energy behind it. Before we even knew what 'sex' meant, we were already plugged into its current. As toddlers, we were curious about our bodies and were often met with panic. 'Don't touch that!' 'That's dirty!'

So, we learnt early that desire equals danger. Curiosity equals guilt. Pleasure equals punishment. And then we grew up wondering why sex makes us feel both free and filthy at the same time. Why we crave touch but fear being seen. Why we chase orgasms but struggle to love ourselves?

At the core, we're not chasing orgasms. We're chasing that fleeting moment when the mind finally shuts up and the body takes over. No performance. No analysis. No mental to-do list. Just presence.

That's why people risk marriages, reputations, and inner peace for it. It's not the person, or the position, or even the orgasm. It's the blackout moment when the ego disintegrates—and for a moment, you experience the bliss of being 'no-thing'.

But like fire, sexual energy either warms the house or burns it down. With awareness, it creates life, art, devotion. Without awareness, it mutates into obsession, addiction, ghosting, love-bombing—in short, the plot summary of your last four situationships.

The good news? Desire isn't the problem. How we relate to it is.

This was Osho's central point. He wasn't merely the bearded provocateur who endorsed free love; he understood that suppressed desire doesn't vanish—it ferments. Shame it, and it becomes guilt, secrecy, and dysfunction. Move with it consciously, and desire becomes a portal.

Attraction comes in many flavours. Sometimes it's raw magnetism. Sometimes it's a shared playlist and existential banter. Sometimes it's the ache in your chest when someone looks at you like home. Sometimes it's all of the above—and suddenly your body is both a temple and a rave.

Each flavour carries its own mirror. If you chase only beauty, the universe will eventually ask: What happens when beauty fades? If you live in the mind, intimacy gets trapped in intellectual foreplay. If you thrive on emotional drama, you'll keep mistaking anxiety for love—until you realise it doesn't have to feel like a roller coaster to be real.

The point isn't to reject these experiences. It's to stop blaming desire when the real disconnect is within. Because most of us aren't actually chasing sex. We're chasing validation—to be seen, chosen, wanted, loved. To quiet the question: *Am I enough?*

When you stop outsourcing your need to feel enough, the whole game changes.

At the highest octave of attraction, the craving for sex itself begins to dissolve. Not in a prudish, 'I've transcended all desire' kind of way, but in a peaceful one. Intensity stops masquerading as intimacy. You no longer need someone else to fill the gaps in your worth.

Sex, it turns out, is the universe's greatest hint.

But just because you know how to flip a light switch doesn't mean you understand electricity. At its highest expression, sex is a doorway to the divine.

And when you finally get it, you realise the G-spot everyone's been searching for is, in fact, the God-spot.

Trigger Me Tender

From the beginning, there was a gnawing unease in my chest. Sharing love hurts. No matter how spiritual you pretend to be, the ego still bruises when it realises it isn't the only one at the table.

I told myself I could handle it—that I wasn't attached to monogamy, that love wasn't a possession. And perhaps I believed it for a while. But beneath that philosophical wallpaper was a sharp, private grief. What stung wasn't merely sharing him—it was being hidden. Tucked away like a secret while he paraded as the dutiful husband.

Before Pondicherry happened, Sankar asked me to work on a play his wife was producing. On paper, it sounded innocent. In reality, the thought of standing before her while knowing what simmered between us made my stomach churn. So, my idealistic, twenty-one-year-old self did what she thought was noble: I reached out and told her the truth—or at least, my version of it. That Sankar and I had grown close, that we'd drawn boundaries and respected them.

She never replied. But he did—with rage. The kind of rage that should've been my cue to exit stage left. Instead, I mistook the red flags for stage curtains and stayed for the next act.

When the physical part of our relationship began, it was intoxicating. Love bombs, attention, fantasies of a shared life. He knew every line in the script. And I, predictably, believed it. But slowly, the curtain began to fall. Missed calls. Delayed messages. Excuses—work, travel, patchy electricity, the ever-present, wife-shaped elephant in the room.

I played the neglected lover, dangling my heartbreak like bait. And he fed on it, because it let him be both saviour and sinner. When that stopped working, I confronted him. And suddenly the roles flipped: He was the victim; I, the villain. Too impatient. Too insecure. Too dramatic. I swallowed those accusations like bitter pills and convinced myself I was the problem.

The only thing I ever truly asked for was honesty. Not labels, not commitment—just the dignity of truth. I told him: 'Tell her. Stop hiding me like I'm something to be ashamed of'.

Each time I brought it up, he Houdini'd his way out—disappearing, deflecting, and blaming. Stories about how fragile she was, how complicated their marriage was, how little I understood. I rationalised, excused, and justified. The constant push and pull left me spiritually seasick. One moment, we were the love of each other's life; the next, we were the source of each other's chaos.

That's when I turned inward. I signed up for a twenty-one-day *Bhairavi Sadhana*, designed to invoke the power of surrender. I threw myself into it completely, and on the final day, I folded all my confusion into one simple prayer: *Let him choose what he wants and end this pain for me. I accept any outcome.*

A few days later, he vanished. No goodbye. No closure. WhatsApp: Blocked. Socials: Deleted. Ghosted, like some Tinder fling—except this one knew the exact coordinates of my soul.

Panicked, I e-mailed him. What came back wasn't closure—it was vitriol. He accused me of exposing our affair to his wife. At first, I was confused, until I pieced it together: My ex in Singapore had decided to sabotage things, dropping truth bombs like a jealous whistleblower.

Sankar's life imploded, and in the rubble, he pointed the finger at me. Given how I'd reached out to her earlier, I couldn't entirely blame him for thinking it might have been me. But he said things I wouldn't repeat even in a drama workshop. Cruel, cutting things designed to erase everything we'd shared.

I was deeply hurt. And in that moment, I couldn't see beyond my own pain.

I knew he'd try to cover his tracks, to spin a story for his wife. But I couldn't let that version stand, not after the things he'd said. I wanted him to face the consequences of his lies. So, I messaged her one last time, offering the truth. She asked for everything—past, present, and future—and I was only too willing to give it to her.

At the time, I told myself I was doing the 'responsible' thing; that I cared about her, and she deserved to know. But really, I was trying to ease my pain, and hand some of it back to them.

Here's the thing: No one warns you what real love looks like. It doesn't glide in with clean fingernails and a five-year plan. It arrives like a wrecking ball, slamming straight into your most deeply buried wounds. The confusion that comes with it isn't dysfunction—it's the curriculum.

That's why we call it *falling* in love. Not strolling. Not gliding. Falling. Because love demands a collapse of the ego. It's a freefall into raw truth. And if you're lucky—or cursed—it either liberates you or wrecks you so completely that you have no choice but to meet yourself.

What Sankar and I had was a spiritual demolition site. He mirrored my deepest wounds: Rejection, abandonment, and the hunger to be seen. I mirrored his: Inadequacy, failure, and the need to be respected. This wasn't romance. It was karmic surgery without anaesthetic.

Everything I thought made me *me*—my likes, dislikes, judgements, biases, opinions, even my moral frameworks—melted into irrelevance. What remained was raw, pulsing truth. Painful, naked, and strangely holy.

That's when I began to understand love. It isn't about holding on. It's about letting go.

THE BODY REMEMBERS

After Sankar, something in me flatlined. I thought rebounds would reboot me—like intimacy was a vending machine: Insert body, select connection, receive wholeness. Instead, every encounter ended the same way. My body folded its arms, shut the blinds, and hung up a sign: Out of service. Try again never.

For months, I wondered if I was broken. At 2 a.m., I found myself googling 'vaginismus'. convinced my body had padlocked the door and switched off the lights. But it wasn't dysfunction. It was memory. The body remembers what the mind tries to bury.

Yogic science has a word for this: *Runanubandha*. It literally means the bonds of body memory. When two people come together—through touch, intimacy, even deep emotional exchange—they don't just swap affection; they swap imprints. This is also the reason behind the traditional gesture of Namaste—it was a yogic way of saying, 'I see your soul, but let's keep our karmas separate.'

Each encounter leaves data in the system. The more often you share, the deeper the groove.

This is why some break-ups sting like a paper cut while others feel like amputation. The more memory you've exchanged, the harder it is to walk away. And this is physics. Every time you make love, you're writing invisible code into each other's bodies. When you separate, the programme doesn't delete—it lingers, running in the background like an app you forgot to close, quietly draining your energy.

But body memory isn't just physical; it's psychological. It blends into what modern psychology calls 'trauma bonding'. When the same person gives you both the wound and the relief, your nervous system wires the two together. Your brain starts craving the very person who caused the pain, in the hope of a fleeting breadcrumb of validation. It's the same mechanism that keeps gamblers hooked to casinos.

On another level, it's also genetic memory. We don't stumble into these patterns by accident; we unconsciously recreate what's familiar.

For example, my father's emotional absence left me chasing after men who withheld. My mother's overgiving—her habit of excusing and even protecting his behaviour—trained me to normalise neglect, accept crumbs as meals, and protect the very people who hurt me. By the time Sankar showed up, my nervous system already knew the choreography: Chase, ache, forgive, repeat.

Ancient cultures understood the stickiness of these bonds, which is why they built rituals for clearing them. In India, the dead are cremated, not buried. And people bathed after funerals or crowded gatherings—not out of superstition, but as energetic hygiene. A dip in water, a fire bath, or even standing in the wind acted as a reset button—a way to clear imprints before they calcified. Science is catching up, too: Water holds memory, carrying vibrations long after the event.

The human body—about 60 per cent water—is a living archive. And my archive was overflowing. Which is why casual encounters felt impossible. My body wasn't punishing me; it was protecting me. Saying: 'We're here to delete the files, not download more.'

The mind will rationalise, romanticise, and insist you can move on. But the body is blunt. It won't fake desire when the imprint still belongs to someone else. And in that way, it becomes your fiercest ally—refusing half-hearted flings, flimsy entanglements, and situationships that leave more residue than joy.

Healing, I've learnt, isn't about forgetting. It's about rewriting the programme through awareness, devotion, discipline, and sometimes just boring old time. Only then does memory stop being a loop and start becoming wisdom.

We like to think we can bury what happened, sweep the mess under the rug, and walk away as if it never existed. That's exactly what Sankar and I tried to do—pretend the connection was an accident instead of an assignment. We refused to do the work it was begging of us because we didn't yet understand the curriculum. We didn't see that we were being called to rewrite the story we were carrying.

But here's the hard truth: Until you do that work, the pattern loops. Runanubandha doesn't allow a quick force-eject. It drags you back, repeatedly, until the debris has burned through and the lessons are learnt.

Which is why, just when I thought it was over, Sankar appeared—again.

Runner & Chaser

Exactly one year after Sankar ghosted me into the digital void, in 2013, an e-mail landed in a forgotten inbox. Sender: Yama Dharmaraj. Only he would pick the god of death to write: 'There's not a moment when I don't think about you. But everything is out of control, so all I do is wish you well. Happy Birthday.'

I was in London at film school, about to fly home for the holidays. On impulse, I replied with a vague itinerary. When I walked out of Mumbai airport a week later, there he was—standing past customs like an apparition. I had no idea where he had come from or where he was headed. We hugged for two minutes, he apologised, and then, true to form, vanished again.

That became the rhythm. Every time I tried to move on, Sankar would reappear like clockwork. I'd dangle a new romantic interest; he'd turn jealous and snarky. We'd talk for a few days, then poof. Gone. Houdini with a side of déjà vu.

Years later, in 2017, he invited me to Singapore to 'heal'. He offered to buy my ticket. I told myself maybe the wound was finally ready to scab over. So, I went.

The week together was anticlimactic. He was defensive, nitpicking my truth. Even the sex felt hollow, like we were re-enacting a play. He dangled promises of a shared life in Singapore, and I—ever the optimist—took up a short-term project there. Within days, he ghosted me again. By then, I had stopped taking his disappearances personally.

Life moved on, but Sankar was never fully gone. By 2022, after pandemic burnout, I had just registered for 'Samyama', Isha's boss-level programme. For the first time, I felt genuinely free of him. I even texted: 'I think you're finally out of my system.' For the first time in years, he replied. His ego could never stomach being erased. And so, within days, we were back in a full-blown affair that felt like 2011 on repeat.

On New Year's Eve 2023, he picked me up at Coimbatore airport and drove me straight to his family jeweller to collect a ring he'd had made for me. The disclaimer was blunt: 'I can't leave my wife, but I'll show up emotionally and promise to do the work.' Almost convincing. But I wasn't the same woman anymore. My trust, once boundless, had frayed. So, I tested him, consciously and unconsciously. And sure enough, the old patterns roared back: Neglect, avoidance, and disrespect.

The bright side? His return gave me just enough fire to quit my toxic job and loveless relationship in Mumbai, and start a new life in Coimbatore, closer to my guru. Poetic, if not healthy. In hindsight, necessary. He had been orbiting every major spiritual milestone, so it almost made sense he was still around when I signed up for Samyama twelve years later.

On the morning of the programme, he even drove me to Isha like the old days. I didn't know it then, but his chaos was the fire I needed to burn through one last layer of delusion. On the third day of Samyama, in complete silence, I saw Sankar's dead body ablaze. It wasn't real, of course, but the vision was so visceral I couldn't escape the emotion as if it were. I had to sit there, unmoving, unable to touch or speak, while my deepest fear rose in front of me: Losing Sankar forever.

What happened after Samyama shook all our delusions from the core. I slowly stopped being afraid of losing him. I started calling out the nonsense instead of swallowing it. When his red flags popped up, I didn't bend or shrink; I challenged his behaviour without spiralling into guilt or self-doubt. I could finally see through the manipulation and the romanticised illusions I had clung to for over a decade.

I could finally see the pattern. And, like any empath with a saviour complex, I wanted to help him. Fix him. Heal him. But the more I tried, the more he ran.

Twelve years earlier, my ex had exposed him to his wife. This time, I did it myself. A part of me was curious to know if he had changed at all. He hadn't. The moment I exposed him, he spewed the same venomous script he had twelve years ago, before vanishing again.

For months, we ran and chased like Tom and Jerry until he finally blocked me everywhere.

Here is the crucial bit: There was something in me that wouldn't stop chasing, no matter how often I said I was done. After a while, instead of shaming myself for it, I got curious. Why was I running after someone who clearly didn't want to be with me? Someone who had proven, over and over, that he couldn't meet me?

Eventually, I realised I wasn't chasing him. I was chasing the part of myself I had abandoned again and again. And once I saw that, the game changed. Because finally, after twelve years of running in circles, I started to see the design.

Karmic Knots

Ever since I moved to Coimbatore, life refused to keep me stationed. Suddenly, I was everywhere, as if the universe had pressed shuffle on my location settings.

At first, I thought it was a string of impulsive trips. But eventually, I caught the pattern. None of these detours was random. Each destination was a karmic knot waiting to be untied, every stop a thread still binding me to Sankar. I felt like Harry Potter on a quest to destroy Horcruxes—except my dark lord was a Tamil theatre director.

Take Munich. On my return from Prague, I had an overnight layover. Logically, I booked a hotel in a suburb near the airport. It was so deserted it felt like the backdrop to a Scandinavian murder series. The thought of spending my first night in Munich there felt criminal. I wanted city lights, bad decisions, and maybe a little techno.

The hotel staff warned me there was a train strike. 'Stay in,' they said. Which, of course, guaranteed I would go out. 90 minutes later, I was still waiting on the platform when an Indian stranger appeared with a power bank to save my dying phone. He even offered to escort me back if transport became a problem. The universe never sends angels in white; it sends them disguised as desi men with charging cables.

My destination was Bahnwärter Thiel, a cultural playground made of graffiti-splashed train carriages stacked like Jenga blocks, pulsing with music and art. But when I got there, I froze. Right next to it was the Münchner Volkstheater—Sankar's main haunt. Above it, a full moon glowed like a spotlight.

In a city this big, on a one-night layover, under a full moon, I 'accidentally' ended up outside *his* place? It felt less like chance and more like choreography. I sat down on a bench, closed my eyes, and exhaled. Just then, something inside unclenched, like a knot I hadn't known I was carrying loosened.

And these accidents kept happening.

Later that year, I found myself at Sadhguru Shri Brahma's ashram in the Nilgiris—a place said to be Sadhguru's playground in a previous lifetime. As I was leaving, a man I'd met there earlier asked if I planned to visit Sadhguru's cave an hour down the hill. I gave a vague 'maybe' and drove off.

Halfway down, I stopped at a plant nursery because my balcony needed more jungle. At checkout, I realised I had no cash and no signal. Just as I was silently cursing my luck, my eyes caught a blue wall with 'Sadhguru' scrawled across it in red paint. I was still wondering what on earth that sign was when I felt a tap on my shoulder.

It was the same man from the ashram with a few other meditators. 'What are you doing here?' he asked, as if I'd been caught trespassing on sacred ground.

'Buying plants? What are you doing here?' I asked, genuinely puzzled. That's when he revealed that I was literally standing at the entrance to Sadhguru's cave—the very one he'd hinted at earlier. Oh, and he happened to have the exact cash I needed to pay for my plants. Of course!

One afternoon, intuition nudged me to check the coordinates of this cave. What I discovered next blew my mind. My home in Coimbatore, Sankar's home, and this cave formed a perfect equilateral triangle. Not approximate—*exact*. Then another triangle revealed itself: My home, his home, and the Isha Yoga Center formed a perfect isosceles. It was as if longitude and latitude themselves were conspiring to sketch the geometry of our karma.

One of my companions on this restless pilgrimage was Prabhu—whose name, in case the universe wanted to be subtle, literally means 'God'. An Isha volunteer with the stamina of a mountain goat, he had a suspicious fondness for leading people up very steep things.

Hiking had never been my thing. I'd always considered myself more of a 'scenic walk and a cup of coffee' person, but after my first trip with Prabhu, I was hooked. Over the next year and a half, I followed him to some truly powerful places. Each time, without fail, the spot would fall into another uncanny triangle connecting me, Sankar, and Sadhguru.

It was as if the universe was guiding me through a cartographic exorcism, using longitude and latitude to loosen the knots between us. Creepy? Absolutely. Effective? Strangely, yes.

The pieces of the puzzle finally started coming together, and I discovered that we were literal mirrors, designed to trigger each other's awakening—not to get married or live happily ever after, but to blow up every illusion we had about life.

Now, even though I knew we'd never 'end up' together, some part of me still wanted to run back and point at everything, to say, 'Look at the design! Isn't it wild?'

I didn't want him back as much as I wanted him to witness what I was witnessing. A last, stubborn flicker of the child who built sandcastles for absent parents, still begging to be seen.

Wishes & Dreams

A part of me still clung to the fantasy that Sankar might awaken. Maybe if I logged enough miles, climbed enough mountains, and whispered enough mantras, the energy would shift. That longing became my secret compass—and it led me to places I never would have gone.

Within a year, I found myself in Kashi, Kedarnath, and finally Kailash. For those who know, these destinations aren't tourist stops; they are summons. You don't just casually 'drop by' Shiva's haunts.

You make it only if he calls.

I have met people who have tried for decades to reach Mount Kailash—money ready, tickets booked, bags packed—only to be turned back by visas, illness, or landslides. And yet, somehow, the road cleared for me as if Shiva had pencilled me into his cosmic calendar.

When Isha announced the annual Kailash–Manasarovar sojourn in 2024, it felt like scoring front-row tickets to Coldplay. I was ready to sell a kidney, but my father saved me from organ donation by sponsoring the trip. My mother and sister joined, too, turning it into a girls-only pilgrimage.

Several groups were travelling that year, but in one of those scheduling twists only the cosmos could choreograph, my group's dates landed us at Kailash on Shivratri itself—the dark moon. On the night of Shiva, we happened to be at the very mountain said to be his abode.

The climb began with sunshine that felt like a blessing. But Shiva is not the kind of host who serves you lemonade and a towel. By afternoon, the skies turned moody: Wind, then rain, then hail sharp enough to sting, and finally snow. By the time we staggered into camp, the mountain had vanished behind a snowstorm.

We had only two nights there, and it seemed likely we'd leave without ever seeing Kailash. But the next day, during a yogic process with a picture of Sadhguru set against the mountain, the sky suddenly cleared. The silence was electric, the air razor-sharp.

That night, under the dark moon, I stood staring up at the Milky Way stretched across the sky. It wasn't merely breathtaking—it was the kind of sight that rearranges your inner furniture.

On impulse, I set my phone on a rock and tried the astrophotography mode I'd never used. Five minutes later, the playback revealed the cosmos in full glory. And then, impossibly, a shooting star streaked across the frame, as if Shiva himself had leaned over to say, 'Make a wish.'

In all these years, Sankar had merely looked at me; never really seen me. But under that frozen sky, I didn't need him to. Because suddenly, I felt seen by Shiva himself . . . Sankar's blind spots no longer mattered.

I had nothing more to wish for—only gratitude for having made it this far.

After Kailash, the universe staged one last knot for me to untie: A family trip to Japan, conveniently disguised as my father's work commitment. Japan was Sankar's karmic playground—his wife was Japanese, his life half-anchored there. On my very first day in Tokyo, in his wife's birthplace no less, I wandered into a shrine at Ueno Park.

The moment I sat down, a monk entered and began to chant as if he had been waiting for me to take a seat. After the prayers, I drifted outside to the wall of wooden plaques where strangers hung their wishes. I had nothing to wish for, but curiosity tugged, so I stopped at one plaque at random.

It read:

> *I pray one day someone chooses you and continues to choose you every day.*
>
> *I pray that someday, all the love you have given will come back to you and stay.*
>
> *And even though today may be filled with tears, I am praying for your joy and happiness.*
>
> *Never forget the light in you, for I know it shines true.*
>
> *And whenever you feel down and not so strong, know that you have been wort*h it all along.

I broke—right there in the middle of Ueno Park—tears blurring the wooden prayers of strangers. It felt as though the universe hadn't just seen me; it had understood me—the ache, the loyalty, the foolish, beautiful persistence of my love.

I hadn't written a wish, but somehow the universe had written one for me.

It felt like a divine reassurance—that the love Sankar had promised me would circle back. I didn't know how or when, but I knew he'd return. And he did—just not in the way I had imagined.

But that, dear reader, is a story for another chapter.

Love Is God

We all grow up believing love is supposed to fix us—that one day, someone will walk in, kiss our chaos into calm, and finally make sense of it all. But the most iconic love stories almost always end in longing, loss, or tragedy. Because love doesn't arrive to complete you; it arrives to compel you to complete yourself.

Nobody proves this better than Shiva and Sati—the original twin flames before it was even a thing. Theirs was never an effortless romance. It was a union was forged in friction, rejection, devotion, and transformation.

Shiva was the ultimate ascetic, the master of detachment who sat for years on end, eyes closed, rejecting all desire. From a modern lens, that's not enlightenment—it's avoidant attachment. Conscious, yet frozen. More knowledge than embodiment.

Then came Sati, the daughter of Daksha. She left her palace, her privilege, and her father's approval for love. Her devotion was total, but so was her desperation. She wanted to be seen by Shiva so badly that she abandoned herself. That's anxious attachment in its most poetic form: All giving, no receiving—performing devotion, hoping it will finally be enough.

When Shiva avoided accompanying her to the Yagna and her father publicly mocked her love, something in her broke. She looked around and realised no one was going to defend her. She decided she was done begging for dignity and walked straight into the fire. People call it sacrifice, but it was, in truth, the moment the feminine declared: I'd rather leave than keep seeking validation from men who refuse to see my worth.

When Shiva lost Sati, that's when he lost his composure. The god who had conquered every plane of existence except the emotional one was forced to feel. For the first time, the lord of stillness trembled. He raged, he wept, he carried her body across the world until even he had to surrender. Awareness finally met emotion.

But love, like life, moves in cycles.

Sati returned as Parvati—a soul tempered by wisdom instead of longing. Shiva was still on his mountain, lost in meditation, eyes closed to the world. So, Parvati turned inward, too, not to prove her love but to purify it. She prayed, practised, and peeled away every trace of the old need for approval. And when she no longer needed him to see her, he finally did.

That was the moment union became possible because both had evolved. Shiva, once the embodiment of detachment, had finally learnt to feel. His awareness, once cold and unyielding, had melted into compassion. And Parvati, who had once mistaken love for approval, had learnt to rest. She no longer performed devotion to be chosen; she had become devotion itself.

When they met again, it wasn't as two halves aching for completion but as two wholes reflecting each other's truth. Stillness met movement. Awareness met emotion. Consciousness finally fell in love with life.

That's the real allegory. We are all Shiva and Sati—avoidant and anxious, ascetic and seeker. One half freezes; the other performs. One intellectualises; the other over-feels. Together, they keep missing each other, trapped in the karmic choreography of their own wounds.

And when we drag those wounds into the dance, love warps. Masculine energy becomes cold, controlling, and unavailable. Feminine energy becomes needy, manipulative, and sacrificial to the point of self-erasure. Because we're not relating from truth; we're relating from trauma.

That's why love feels brutal. It's not here to hand you the perfect partner; it's here to expose your patterns. Every heartbreak, every push–pull cycle, every karmic cliff-dive with someone who smells like regret and sandalwood isn't punishment—it's initiation.

Love is the universe's most seductive form of shadow work.

And here's the secret nobody likes to admit: The deepest loves are designed *not* to work. Because love is easier in the absence than in the presence. When they're gone, you're left alone with your projections, your fantasies, and your ache. That's when the real questions surface: Was I in love with them, or just the way they made me feel? Were they my soulmate, or merely the mirror that showed me my own longing?

This is why mystics tell us to fall in love with God or the guru. The divine doesn't breadcrumb, ghost, or leave you on 'seen'. You love for love's sake, not for validation. And in that one-way devotion, something alchemical happens—the fantasy dissolves, the self heals, and love evolves from possession to presence.

But let's be honest: Not everyone is built to swoon over a formless void or a man in robes. That's why creation, in its trademark mischief, gave us lovers instead—messy, magnetic, infuriating humans who touch your hand one moment, trigger your childhood trauma the next, and somehow still teach you more about divinity than any scripture ever could.

That's the paradox of love. You think you're searching for 'the one', but they're not here to complete you—they're here to stretch you to the edge of your ego until you crack open and your love evolves into its highest expression: Compassion.

Finally, the lover was never the destination. They were only the doorway to the divine.

SOLULU 5

Commit to Love

They say love is blind, but it's the only thing that will slap your third eye wide open.

The truth is, most of us flirt with life. We dabble, we sample, we 'vibe check' everything—from careers to relationships to spiritual paths—terrified of giving ourselves fully to anything in case it doesn't love us back, or worse, leaves us. But love doesn't work like a dating app. You can't scroll your way into transformation. You have to pick something and commit.

And this is what marriage was meant to be. Not a contract for security, status, or survival, but a sacred container for ego death. A structure designed to help two people burn through their illusions together—to hold up mirrors to each other's blind spots and rise into wholeness side by side. But somewhere along the way, marriage was hijacked by transaction. It became less about liberation and more about possession. That's why when a marriage stops working, it's not a failure; it's an exposure. It reveals the illusion it was built on.

Commitment isn't about another person; it's about your own integrity. In fact, it doesn't even have to be a person. It just needs to be something that keeps calling to you: A passion, a purpose, a practice. Whatever it is, don't ghost it when things get hard. Because they will get hard. You'll doubt it, resent it, and question whether it was ever meant for you. That's the moment most people run. But the 'solulu' is to stay.

Stay when the discomfort begins. Stay when the fantasy dissolves. Stay until you're dragged through the gritty back alleys of your own resistance, until something in you finally breaks. Commitment isn't about martyrdom or appearances; it's about staying long enough to burn through your illusions. And yes, there may come a time to leave. But you'll only know it's time when you're no longer acting from ego or fear, but from clarity.

Everything you chase will eventually test your commitment to it. If it's money, you'll probably lose it and have to rebuild. If it's fitness, you'll be forced to rest just when you start seeing abs. If it's a person, they'll leave, betray, or disappoint you. And if you think renouncing the world and becoming a monk will spare you this lesson, prepare to meet yourself on the monastery bathroom floor at 3 a.m.

But here's the divine trick: Through the loss, the crumbling, and the unbearable ache of not getting what you want, you'll be forced to detach —and led straight to what you actually need. *Yourself.* This is where the narrative of romantic love begins to fall apart. Love, in its truest form, doesn't show up to complete you; it shows up to awaken you to complete yourself.

When you stop looking for someone else to fill your cup and start learning how to fill your own, that cup begins to overflow. And from that overflowing cup, when you give love without expectation, that's when everything and everyone starts loving you back.

It is through this process that you will understand the laws of the universe and come face to face with the source of creation.

That's why they said Love is God.

Delulu 6

I AM SOMEBODY

'You are not here to prove your worth.

You are here to live.'

- Thich Nhat Hahn

Role Play

The cosmic joke is this: After all the heartbreak, the chasing, the karmic soap operas dressed up as love stories, you don't get to keep the person. You don't even get to keep the fantasy of the person. What you're left with is . . . you. And that's when it hits: Maybe you weren't just searching for love. Maybe you were searching for identity.

Because love has never been only about being wanted. It's been about being somebody. Fighting for the right to say: I'm somebody's girlfriend. Somebody's husband. Somebody's boss. Somebody's child. Somebody who matters. God forbid we wake up without a label to hold on to. Who would we even be? Just a human being? Ew. No, thanks!

Once upon a time, identity was simple. You were the blacksmith's son, the baker's daughter, the warrior, the healer, the midwife. Function was identity. End of story.

Then modernity showed up like a zealous director. The Renaissance handed us 'the Self', postmodernism gave us 'reason', and capitalism gave us 'LinkedIn'. Suddenly, identity wasn't inherited—it was performed, built, branded, marketed, and sold.

Our obsession with being somebody didn't fall from the sky. It was programmed in. From childhood, we were asked the most conditioning question of all: 'What do you want to be when you grow up?'

> Not *who* do you want to be?
> Not *how* do you want to feel?
> *What.* A noun. A title. A box to crawl into.

> And it doesn't stop at childhood. It just keeps morphing:
> Who are you?
> What do you do?
> What have you achieved?
> What's your five-year plan?
> Where do you see yourself?

The Industrial Revolution turned us into cogs, but the Digital Revolution taught us to brand the cog. It's now a cultural epidemic where our worth is directly proportional to our LinkedIn headline, our wedding hashtag, our number of followers, or our ability to recite our job title without crying.

We are a generation who can list our Myers–Briggs type, moon sign, attachment style, sexual preferences, and pronouns faster than we can name our friends—because friends don't define us anymore; our statuses and labels do.

We measure success in blue ticks and corporate ladders. We measure love in couple selfies and engagement rings. We measure spiritual progress by how many retreats we've cried at. We're expected to self-market at all times and become somebody, so that the world knows where to place us.

Because being nobody—just existing without a tagline—is our biggest collective fear. And so, we build identities like IKEA furniture: Jobs, relationships, degrees, awards, diagnoses, and curated aesthetics, all bolted together just enough to say, 'See? I matter.' Even if it's wobbly as hell and missing half the screws.

Sociologists call it 'identity capital', the collection of achievements and affiliations we accumulate to prove our value to the world. But beneath it, though, is pure panic. The quiet terror of being ordinary; of not having a label impressive enough to silence our self-doubt.

Our culture doesn't just reward becoming somebody; it punishes anyone who dares to opt out. You don't want to marry or have children? Enjoy the unsolicited lectures on loneliness and osteoporosis. You dropped your corporate title to follow your bliss? Congrats! Now you're a 'freelancer', which is capitalist code for unemployed until proven otherwise.

Titles become armour. Strip them away, and what's left is the thing society fears most: A raw, label-less human, still fumbling towards meaning. And nothing terrifies the world more than a person who refuses to pick a lane and stay there.

The Imposter's Stage

The societal pressure to *be somebody* was real. I'm not going to sit here and pretend I was floating around on some Zen cloud while the rest of the world played Monopoly with degrees and careers. I was fully subscribed to the hustle, operating from my deepest insecurities.

Despite being the star student in film school—both in undergrad and postgrad—I carried around my imposter syndrome like it was a designer handbag, matching it perfectly with my ambitions and crippling self-doubt. Deep down, I knew I had managed to coast through years of formal education while remaining remarkably uneducated.

I didn't understand half the obscure film references my classmates tossed around. I hadn't watched the classics. I couldn't fake enthusiasm for French black-and-white existential crises that bored me to death. I didn't know my Godard from my Tarkovsky—and honestly, I didn't care. But it left me feeling smaller. Less talented. Less deserving of a seat at the 'serious film-maker' table.

Screenwriting and fiction gave me hives. The thought of coming up with an idea, rewriting drafts, setting a scene, lighting it, blocking it, casting actors, and directing them—all in service of an elaborate lie—was exhausting. Which is why I gravitated towards documentaries. No need to make anything up; just tell it as it is. And when questioned, I'd play the morally superior card while my ego did a little victory dance. The reality? I was lazy.

Sure, a part of me wanted the glamour—the mainstream film industry, red carpets, awards, and validation wrapped in sequins. But if I were being honest, I was terrified of fiction because I didn't know how to imagine. So, for my graduation film, I stayed where it felt safe: Documentary. And because I still wanted a little glamour to prove I wasn't wasting my tuition fees, I made a film with Shah Rukh Khan as my lead. No joke.

Around that time, *Dilwale Dulhania Le Jayenge* was all over the news for completing a 1,000-week uninterrupted run at Mumbai's Maratha Mandir, making it the longest-running film in history. *Bam!* The universe had handed me the perfect subject. Nostalgic, iconic, and impossible to mess up. I wasn't reinventing cinema; I was documenting a phenomenon people already adored. It felt like the perfect hack.

The process of making the film was my own little MBA in negotiation, publicity, and bulldozing through red tape. Yash Raj Films doesn't exactly hand out permissions like Diwali sweets, but I somehow pulled it off. I went from being the insecure film student who couldn't light a scene to the first person in sixty years of London Film School to negotiate shared rights on a student film. I wasn't just making a film—I was making institutional history.

But I didn't stop there. I crafted my own press release, pitched myself to editors like I was my own agent, hustled my way into coverage by major publications globally, and trended in the top ten on Twitter before the film was even made. I even gave a live interview on BBC Radio. Imagine this: A student talking about her film before the film even existed. Unheard of. Ridiculous. A little bit iconic, if we're being honest.

And when I finally did make it, of course, I wasn't happy with the outcome. But people loved it anyway. The film got attention, it screened at the Barbican as part of the London Film School's annual showcase, and it made it to several festivals. Ten years later, in 2025, it's *still* being screened at festivals. From the outside? Total success. From the inside? I felt like a fraud—not necessarily because of the film, but because of what I had become to make it happen.

For years, I told myself the story: *I couldn't achieve my artistic vision because I was too busy directing and producing it.* But deep down, I knew the truth was messier. I had a very capable producer who worked incredibly hard, but I didn't trust her. I micromanaged her into oblivion. When she finally distanced herself from the project, I blamed her for everything that hadn't gone to plan and even took her credit away.

Honestly, the London chapter of my life—great as it was—was a cocktail of shame and insecurity, with the Ziad episode on the personal front and this on the academic. On paper, I was *somebody*, but in reality, recognition wasn't enough to silence the voice in my head that still whispered: *You're a fraud.*

It was 2016, and I returned to India after graduation feeling like I'd been chewed up and spat out by ambition, love, and my own illusions. My confidence was shattered, and as always, I turned to spirituality like a boomerang returning to its favourite crutch. I registered for a twenty-one-day detox at the Isha Yoga Center, hoping for a hard reset—it had always worked before.

There I was after my detox programme: Fresh off the mat, fresh out of tears, fresh into another attempt at 'starting over'. I accepted a project to film a documentary for a non-profit. I thought it would be humble, grounding—a good restart.

But life, as usual, had other plans. Little did I know another curveball was about to knock the breath out of me and disorient the absolute crap out of my carefully constructed *somebody* identity.

THE OPENING ACT

From max-glam graduation screenings in London straight to the grassroots chaos of India. Honestly? I was relieved. After the ego parade of celebrity interviews and creative politics that revolved around who got the most applause, this felt like penance. I was trading my inner diva for my inner documentarian—serving, observing, redeeming.

The project was simple: Film a week-long community arts project for local children. Less red carpet, more dust and heat. Beneath the sweat, a small part of me felt cleansed. Here I was, back to basics. No studio, no ego, just children, art, and the camera between us.

Then she walked in.

The woman at the helm. A magnetic presence, sharp-eyed and self-assured in a way that instantly disarmed me. Not the glossy kind of beautiful, but compelling in a way that pulled people into her orbit. Within minutes, I'd clocked the hierarchy: she was the Queen Bee, I was the worker.

Her story matched the aura—an artist and activist who had survived an abusive marriage. Naturally, I googled her. The more

I read, the more I admired her. My insecurity morphed into ambition. I wanted her to notice my brilliance. Instead, she looked right through me.

On the final day, I finally got my moment: interviewing her. That's when she saw me—not as furniture, but as someone worth talking to. I mentioned my spiritual leanings, hoping to impress her. To my surprise, she didn't blink. She, too, had been initiated by Sadhguru years ago, although she had never been to the yoga centre. Funny, the little overlaps life loves to script.

A month later, she was visiting Mumbai and invited me to breakfast. I pulled out my best 'grown-up' energy and, in a moment of questionable judgement, spilt my heartbreak story about Sankar. She mirrored me with one of her own—a Tamil Brahmin who had left her crying on the bathroom floor for three days. *Trauma twins*, I thought.

We spent the day together, and I gave her an observation-deck tour of my life. She wanted to make a film about children and resilience. Writing was her gift; production was mine. It felt like the universe had answered my prayers—a writer, delivered on a silver platter. Desperate to impress, I whipped up a pitch deck and production timeline faster than you could say 'people pleaser', performing competence like an art form.

Somewhere in this unfolding dynamic, I mentioned my plans to visit Isha for a dark moon ritual at the Dhyanalinga Temple. She wanted to come and asked if she could bring another woman. Sure, I said, imagining myself as her spiritual concierge. Only on the flight did I realise that 'friend' was her long-time partner.

Last-minute plans being the cosmic pranksters they are, we wound up sharing a room. And just like that, I was thrust into the private world of a same-sex couple in their fifties—a whole new territory.

Preparing for the dark moon ritual, I shaved my head alongside the monks—a symbolic shedding of the old and reclaiming the tomboyish freedom I'd once known, before society handed mea script titled 'How to Be a Woman Without Making Anyone Uncomfortable'.

Interestingly, my story with Sankar had begun on a Full Moon during a ritual honouring the 'Divine Feminine'. Now, exactly seven years later, I was with Queen Bee on the dark moon, bowing to the 'Divine Masculine'. The dance of polarities was already in motion; I hadn't yet caught on.

When the trip ended, her partner—rarely one to host outsiders—invited me to their city . . . and to their home. Even Queen Bee's children weren't welcomed in that space, so this felt like a big deal. I felt chosen. Special.

A few weeks later, while filming in Goa, I received an invitation to watch her play. She insisted I fly in. Without hesitation, I booked my flight, found a replacement for my shoot, and arrived at midnight. A driver took me straight to her workspace, where she was neck-deep in production chaos.

Her funding had fallen through, deadlines loomed, and she was musing about selling belongings to keep the show afloat. Odd, I thought, for someone radiating such power. But I'm naïve. I slipped into fixer mode, found a last-minute sponsor, and saved the night.

Hero entry unlocked.

Back at her home, I noticed something curious. Though she and her partner shared a life, they lived in separate rooms. With only two rooms available, I was meant to share hers . . . and her bed.

That night after the show, something shifted. It felt like Sankar in the tent all over again. Inexplicable. Magnetic. I found myself attracted to this older woman in a way I'd never anticipated. My straight-as-an-arrow track record didn't align with these newfound desires creeping up on me.

My body, as always, gave me away—tight chest, trapped gas, the usual anxiety symphony. When she offered to hold me 'like a child', I didn't resist. What followed was baffling, electric, familiar in a way logic couldn't decode.

The next morning, I woke up to find her watching me the same way Sankar once had. I blurted, half-joking, 'I think you're turning me gay.' She burst into a snorty guffaw, brushing it off as youthful confusion. She made it clear she intended only to collaborate professionally. She spoke about her abusive past and her dreams of revenge-fuelled fame as a screenwriter and director.

Perfect, I thought. She might not want me, but she had the stories, and I had the production skills. Together, we could create something powerful.

Deep down, I also wanted her love and adoration—to be seen, to be chosen. So, what if she was already committed? I'd made unavailable people fall for me before. So, what if she thought I was just a child? I would show her my depth.

From that moment, it wasn't so much about the collaboration as it was about making her see me.

And here is where things got complicated. Because eventually, she did see me—better than I could see myself.

Before I knew it, our grand film plans were sidelined when she decided to stage a play—a high-stakes, low-budget gamble. Unemployed, insecure, and eager to matter, I followed her everywhere—meetings, rehearsals, brainstorms—like an eager tail wagging behind its master.

She had a gift for sliding into people's lives and making herself indispensable. One day, she'd charm producers into lending us a rehearsal space; the next, she'd convince some eager-to-matter guy to sponsor the show. Except, in every meeting, there was always a side huddle I wasn't invited to—quiet negotiations, whispered alliances.

Once, one of the producers casually referred to 'the three of us'—meaning themselves and her—as if I were invisible. When I confronted her, she laughed it off: 'Oh, they're married, so they count as one.' Technically, clever. Morally, shady.

That was our first fight, and the first red flag I pretended was a fairy light. Why I stayed was layered: part attraction, part saviour complex, part delusion that she was my ticket to relevance. She saw it clearly—my hunger, my desperation, my need to prove I was a somebody.

Somehow, we pulled it off. The premiere was glossy enough to draw some local attention, but financially, it was a trainwreck. Sponsors vanished, partners ghosted, and suddenly it was just the two of us, registering a company together as if paperwork could save us.

Professionally, things were cooling. Personally? Not so much.

By then, I had seduced her, and we were in a full-blown, physically intimate affair. She had told her partner about me. Unsurprisingly, her partner wasn't thrilled. But I was glad she wasn't pulling a Sankar on me. No secret texts. No ghosting marathons. I wasn't even bothered that I had to share her. Hell, I wasn't even sure what 'this' was. It was my first time in Lesbian County, and the maps weren't clear.

Then came a film festival where my DDLJ documentary was screening, and she tagged along. In a moment of Bollywood-level melodrama, she confessed she was in love with me—ready to upend her life and move in together. It had been six months since I'd known her and four since I'd even realised I wasn't as straight as I thought. I told her the truth: I wasn't ready. Not for her, not for anyone.

Cue the drama. Overnight, I became the betrayer.

In hindsight, she wasn't entirely wrong. I had seduced her into believing this was more, only to flinch when it demanded commitment. A part of me had wanted control after all the times she'd made me feel small. But power built on pain always collapses.

Then, in a twist that came out of nowhere, a lucrative corporate offer brought me to her city—five-star suite, car, laundry, gourmet meals—the kind of package people twice my age were still chasing. I said yes. And just like that, fate dragged me straight to her backyard.

Of course, we reconnected. On paper, we were still 'partners' in our company, developing creative projects. She dreamed, I decked and pitched. But chemistry doesn't respect contracts. It leaked into every exchange. Slowly, she began to pull away physically. At first, I couldn't understand it. Now I see it for what it was—self-preservation. She'd already been burned once.

But the more she withdrew, the more I chased. That old toxic choreography: Distance, pursuit; withdrawal, surrender. Until she softened. Until I did, too.

I lasted four months in the corporate bubble. Despite the perks, the people and the performance drained me dry. Eventually, I quit.

And, of course, she was there—waiting, ready to pull me back into whatever vortex we had been spinning all along.

By then, things had shifted for her within the non-profit she was running. All I knew was that wherever she was, I would follow. Whether it was love, ambition, the desperate need to feel seen and validated, or all of it at once, I wasn't done yet.

Dress Rehearsal

She wasn't running an NGO as much as resuscitating one. Once a force in social reforms, it now limped on nostalgia and unpaid bills. But by the time I met her, she was ready to pull the plug and reinvent herself as a writer. That workshop where we met? Supposed to be her grand finale.

What I didn't see then was the frustration simmering beneath her decision. For years, she had been fighting for policy access, pushing for educational reform, trying to spare children the trauma she had lived. Yet, every door stayed shut.

The plot twist, as divine timing would have it, came as soon as I left my cushy job. The long-awaited government mandate she had been waiting for arrived. They wanted us to run a programme for Indian youth, but of course, without the money. To her, it was a sign. 'This is perfect,' she told me. 'No money means no interference. Total creative freedom.'

Or total delusion? TBD.

She sold me the dream: We would raise independent funds and roll out a nationwide youth movement to prevent gender-based violence. We would still pursue our creative projects in our spare time. But this mission was her real fight.

To be fair, she was always clear: 'Join because you want to. Not because of me.' But her actions told a different story. Deadlines flew at me like dodgeballs in PE class. Websites had to be built overnight. Decks in five hours. Proposals needed to land on desks yesterday. Everything was urgent. Life or death.

And because I was who I was—recovering people-pleaser, overachiever, chronic saviour complex in a cute jumpsuit with bags of childhood wounds and unresolved trauma—I became her one-person army. I saw her vision, passion, exhaustion, and need. I saw that, without money or manpower, she needed me. And wasn't that what I wanted? To feel needed? Important? Part of something bigger than myself? So, I stayed.

To add another twist, she roped in the same eager-to-matter sponsor from our ill-fated theatre production. Despite burning himself previously, he convinced his business partner to jump on this ship and even recruited his young son. We weren't just building a programme; we were building a movement. Or so we told ourselves, over and over again, like a delusion we couldn't afford to break.

Given our creative backgrounds, she seeded another idea: A for-profit wing to fund the non-profit dream. We'd sell services—communications, strategy, content—to keep the mission afloat. Although it sounded noble and inspiring, it also sounded exhausting. But I was already in too deep.

Naturally, my parents were concerned about my career, my future, and this older woman who seemed to have me under a spell. They didn't know the half of it—not the emotional entanglement, not the blurred lines.

At the start of all this, she joined my family for a programme at Isha. Smart move. Nothing earns Indian parents points like spiritual tourism. She knew which card to play: Spirituality softens suspicion. Even so, my parents weren't fooled. Polite, but wary from day one.

They warned me. Yet, I kept playing.

The day we finally made our first real profit from the 'for-profit' side, she encouraged me to donate every rupee I had earned as my personal fee. She had donated hers, she said. This was how we would build something 'together as equal partners'. Shared sacrifice for a higher cause. And so, this became the template for every project.

I had no money anyway. I didn't need it. I was living in my parents' house, relying on their support, trying to outrun the growing shame of being an overqualified, unpaid intern in my own life. But what I did have was ambition, hunger, and an endless need to prove myself. That's what she played. Not cruelly. Just instinctively.

Publicly, I was Director of Communications. Privately, I was her workhorse. I built the infrastructure, activated networks, brought in people, and got things done. Every time I spoke up about feeling invisible, she'd soothe me with admiration. 'You're magic,' she'd say, eyes soft, voice honeyed. High on validation, I'd push harder. Bring more people in. Work longer hours.

Eventually, with all the contributions I was making and the respect I wasn't getting, I finally demanded a seat at the table. On paper, I was somebody. In reality, the table was still hers.

Once I joined the board, there was no leaving. We spent money we didn't have on her travel. I couldn't keep working from my parents' house, so we rented an apartment—a quiet leafy place with a sliver of sea—which became our office, our home, and our trap. I wasn't paid, but I was grateful for a roof over my head, purpose in my days, and the illusion of building something meaningful. That gratitude kept me blind longer than it should have.

At the start, I had charmed her. But now the tables had turned. She'd started playing me. Consciously or not, who's to say? She saw the parts of me I hadn't dared to see myself. She knew exactly which strings to pull. Soon, I caught on. I figured her Achilles' heel was her need to feel desired. So, I used it to keep my own leverage intact. We were both manipulating. We were both surviving.

Meanwhile, the cracks widened. We juggled both for-profit and non-profit work with no funding, no full-time staff, no systems. Already exhausted from the toxicity of our relationship and the chaos of our daily hustle, she kept saying yes to more colleges, more projects, more clients. We spread ourselves thinner than cheap butter on dry toast. I was clocking fourteen- to eighteen-hour days, surviving on caffeine and cortisol.

Somewhere along the way, I started wondering if her hyper-productivity was a trauma response. Perhaps she wasn't driven. Maybe she was running. I didn't have the language back then, just resentment and fatigue.

Whenever I complained that we weren't working on the creative projects we'd once dreamed of, she'd add more projects to the pile. I kept pitching anyway, and once, one of our ideas even got optioned by an Academy Award-winning producer. For five minutes, it felt like we'd made it. But then it fizzled, like everything else.

Finally, through one of my contacts, we landed our first major grant. We could hire staff. After two years of unpaid labour, we started drawing salaries—Rs 25,000 a month—less than my father's chauffeur.

To lighten the load, I hired interns and entry-level executives, paying them next to nothing but selling them the same dream I'd bought into. I became a mini version of her—motivating, manipulating, and romanticising hustle culture. When they underperformed, I snapped. They'd quit, burnt out, disgruntled, sometimes retaliating with vengeance. She'd cut off their access, withhold payments, and we'd hire a fresh batch. The toxic cycle looped.

Somehow, it was always my fault. In board meetings, she was calm and rational. I was the emotional one. My health collapsed. My spiritual practice evaporated. I stopped seeing my family. I had no friends outside work. I was isolated, tired, bitter, spiralling.

But she wasn't on a pedestal watching me burn. She was burning, too. Equally exhausted, stretched, drowning. This made it harder to stop. If she was breaking herself for the mission, who was I to complain? This was the same script I handed down to our staff: If we suffer together, surely that's solidarity. Not dysfunction.

At one point, her body gave out. A chain of health crises followed. We turned to my father—the man who had never trusted her but still honoured his oath as a doctor.

For the first time, fear hit me. Not just fear for her life. Fear for me. What happens if she isn't here to steer this ship? What would happen to the mission, to the people dependent on us, to the monster I had fused so tightly with my own worth?

By then, I was in too deep. Way too deep to walk away. And she—ever perceptive—had already sniffed out my greatest fear.

BREAK-A-LEG

It is poetic, in a cruel way. An organisation built to prevent violence slowly became the most emotionally violent space I'd ever known. Irony really is the universe's favourite punchline.

But this is how trauma plays out, isn't it? We unconsciously repeat what we've survived. Hurt people hurt people—sometimes softly, in the name of love. Sometimes brutally, in the name of justice. Sometimes so blindly, they genuinely believe they're helping. Queen Bee was living proof.

I wasn't immune either. I thought I was helping. I thought I was saving the world. In truth, I was repeating the very violence I'd been dealt—passing it down to staff, interns, anyone within reach. What we don't heal, we hand over. That's the fine print nobody tells you.

Still, I'm grateful for the clarity it carved into me. Pain became my portal. Exhaustion, my teacher. Without her, I might never have seen myself so starkly.

For one, I was forced to confront my internalised misogyny. Generations of women before me had taught me to distrust, even resent, other women. Working under one so unapologetically powerful, complicated, and chaotic cracked something open. It healed something fundamental between me and the feminine.

I also came face-to-face with my lack mentality. She spent money like it was water; I hoarded it like fossil fuel. Her recklessness terrified me, but it also taught me abundance is more about trust than numbers—a trust I didn't yet have, not even in myself.

Of course, there were textbook lessons, too. I learnt feminism, gender laws, human rights, and the history of resistance. I studied how power functions, how violence is systemic, how cycles repeat. But all of that was theory. The real education was living inside the experiment—being both subject and perpetrator in a case study of my own making.

I learnt how to hustle. How to build an organisation from scratch—systems, operations, fundraising, PR. Not because I was prepared, but because she threw me in without floaties. Sink or swim. Turns out, I could swim. Not gracefully, but enough to get us to shore.

I also learnt how the world works. How people are manipulated. How awards are bought. How optics are curated like museum exhibits. Impact, I realised, is often a pie chart on a presentation, not a transformation in a life. And love? Love was the grandest illusion of all.

Once, while retrieving a file from her phone, curiosity betrayed me. I saw her chat with her partner. The same photo of her tea. The same, 'Miss you. Love you.' Sent to both of us. Copy, paste. It wasn't even elaborate—just lazy duplicity. Neither of us was special enough to deserve our own lie.

And yet, I convinced myself I was important. Our organisation felt like the centre of the universe. I resented anyone who didn't see the 'magnitude' of our work. I judged those who didn't care enough, donate enough, or speak up enough. My pedestal grew taller and my delusion thicker. I collected more certificates, awards, accolades—more proof to outrun the shame of the absolute fraud I felt like.

Over time, our fights grew more toxic. She withdrew the attention my ego fed on, and without it, my motivation soured. I accused her of using me. She denied it. But the truth sat between us like smoke: We were both using each other. Feeding off wounds. Playing out patterns. Mirroring back the worst parts of ourselves with brutal precision.

But she sowed the seed of an important lesson I would learn one day: Emotional accountability. Every time I said I loved her, she wanted a list of reasons why. Every time I upset her, she didn't want apologies. She wanted specifics. A breakdown of my crime, point by point. Exactly how had I hurt her? What was the impact of my actions? Where had my words landed?

I tried. I really did. I sat there, wracking my brain like a student facing an exam they hadn't revised for because they didn't even know the subject existed. I wasn't intentionally being an asshole. I genuinely just couldn't see it. My awareness hadn't yet stretched wide enough to meet the version of myself she kept handing back to me.

The sheer exhaustion from trying to stand on emotional ground I hadn't yet built within myself felt like punishment then. Now, I see it for what it was: Practice for the accountability life would eventually demand of me. Practice for the day, I'd stop defending myself long enough to witness myself.

But that day didn't come with her. It came way after I left. That's when I understood what she'd been trying to teach me. Emotional accountability isn't about intentions; it's about impact. It's learning to sit with the ways we hurt others, even when we didn't mean to.

Eventually, the fatigue of trying to keep up with her truth swallowed me whole. Each time I asked to resign, blaming her leadership style for my misery, she would play me on my greatest fear—call a board meeting, threaten to resign herself, and leave the whole organisation in my lap. She knew exactly how much that terrified me.

By then, over a hundred people depended on us. I wasn't equipped to lead them. And besides, this wasn't even the life I wanted. But I was broke, comfortable in the pretty house, and terrified of failing on my own. So, I stayed each time.

There was high-octane drama almost every month. And after all that, she'd look at me, calm as a Buddha after a bender, and say: 'Thank you for being my teacher.'

Teacher? Back then, I couldn't see it. I couldn't see anything through the fog of exhaustion, fear, and projection. But she could. She saw something I hadn't yet caught up to.

Behind the Character

For years, I couldn't understand why, after twelve years of domestic violence, she never pressed charges against her ex-husband. No alimony, no legal battle, no dragging him through the mud. She just packed up her children, walked out with nothing, lived in the slums, and rebuilt her life from scratch. Alone.

When I asked her why, her answer was disarming in its simplicity: 'There's no point fighting battles you can't win. In court, anything can be proven. Besides, I wasn't innocent either.'

At first, it sounded like resignation. But over time, I realised she'd grasped something most of us never do: People aren't villains or victims. They're teachers. Each heartbreak, each betrayal carries a curriculum. Her ex-husband was part of hers. And while she may have seen the design, I don't think she fully accepted it. She let go of the court case, not because she truly surrendered, but because she knew she couldn't win.

A part of her still desperately wanted to win.

When I looked closer at my own situation with her, I had to admit—it wasn't that different. Yes, I could catalogue the ways I'd been hurt, undermined, and manipulated. But I wasn't innocent either. I mirrored the very behaviours I condemned—controlling, blaming, chasing validation like it was oxygen.

At one point, I started googling 'narcissism' to understand her. Five clicks later, I was diagnosing myself. Before I knew it, I was wearing 'narcissist' as a name tag. Shame became my identity. But every time I spiralled, she'd tell me, 'Be kinder to yourself. You're not seeing the full picture.'

The irony was unbearable. Empathetic in theory; cold in practice. Preaching empowerment while running an organisation on the fumes of victimhood. That gap confused me most: how someone who had lived through so much suffering could still be hell-bent on punishing those who didn't bend to her will.

Then I stumbled across a new term: 'Dark Empath'. Empathy sharpened into a weapon. Kindness, a tool for control. Suddenly, everything made sense. She wasn't a contradiction; she was a category. Box ticked. Case closed.

Except . . . boxes are for storage, not for souls.

The truth is, narcissism isn't some fringe disorder—it's a cultural epidemic. We live in a world that preaches self-care but rewards self-interest, where even kindness gets monetised. Sure, some people are better at the performance than others, but the hunger underneath is the same. The need to be seen, chosen, special. That ache isn't a diagnosis; it's the basis of the human condition. No label can heal it.

Psychology might help us see the pattern, give us labels, frameworks, maybe even temporary relief—but it can't free us. Beneath every behaviour is a soul curriculum. The soul doesn't sign contracts for pleasure alone. It signs up for pain, too. For the betrayals that strip you, the illusions that burn you, the lovers that undo you—not to punish, but to awaken. Osho said it best: 'Psychology is not enough. What we need is a metapsychology.'

Looking back, I can see how I mistook labels for clarity. Leader. Activist. Film-maker. Gender-fluid. Demisexual. Narcissist. Survivor. Each identity felt like a breakthrough, a doorway into my truth. But instead of doors, they became walls. The more tightly I defined myself, the smaller I became. And in boxing myself in, I boxed everyone else, too.

Human beings are not boxes. We are contradictions. We are shifting weather—masculine one moment, feminine the next. Brave and terrified in the same breath. We're not nouns, we're verbs. Rivers that flood, dry out, change course, and carve new banks. But the ego clings to 'somebody-ness' like survival depends on it. We build shrines to our identities and call it progress.

Take even the noblest labels. The gender pronoun 'they/them' was meant to unite, to soften boundaries. And yet, listen closely: *They, them* still point outward. It still says, 'I am not you.' The intention is inclusion, but the outcome is another layer of separation. Words can't bridge a gap the heart refuses to cross.

Through all of this, something in me began to dissolve. My craving for validation fell away. My gender blurred. Masculine, feminine, straight, queer—none of it felt relevant anymore. My body felt less like identity, more like a vehicle. I wasn't a label. I wasn't a role. I was consciousness moving through a curriculum I'd signed up for long before I landed here.

And that was the joke the universe had been trying to tell me all along.

The more I peeled back the layers of memory, the more I began to remember who I truly was—and who we all are beneath the costume changes. The deeper I went, the clearer it became that what we call 'homosexuality' or 'gender fluidity' isn't a deviation or a disorder—it's memory. It's the soul remembering a love it has known before, a sacred contract carried across time and space.

Often, the reason a person doesn't feel at home in their own gender has nothing to do with confusion—it's continuity. The memory of being another gender or a wound of being a particular gender in another lifetime is still alive in their field, like an echo that hasn't faded. The body may have changed, but the imprint of that identity still lingers in the soul's data.

There are no mistakes in how we are born. Every detail—body, gender, orientation, temperament—is part of the soul's design. The module is perfect, even when it's uncomfortable. It's all engineered to help us remember that we are not these roles, but the awareness playing through them.

And when you truly see that, the labels fall away. There is no 'straight' or 'queer', no 'he', 'she', or 'they', no 'narcissist' or 'empath'. There is only consciousness, exploring itself through every possible form.

We are the dance of Shiva and Shakti within a single breath—two forces, eternally entwined, remembering they were never separate to begin with.

THE DANCE OF DUALITY

The reason so many queer people get triggered when someone smugly declares, 'There are only two genders' is because, annoyingly, it's kind of true. Not in the checkbox-on-a-passport sense, but in the grander, cosmic-architecture sense.

Strip away the buffet of labels we've crafted to feel seen, and life moves through two primal currents: Masculine and Feminine. Shiva and Shakti. Yin and Yang. These polarities have nothing to do with the body you were born with or your freedom to love another human being.

The reason some straight folks squirm when queer people say 'love is love' is because . . . well, that's true, too. Love doesn't care about gender. It isn't bound by chromosomes or social categories. It just wants to merge—sometimes with a person, sometimes with a tree, sometimes with the sky.

The ego craves certainty. The soul craves union.

Queer people live this paradox most intimately. We are the bridge between binaries, the space where energies blur and refuse to sit neatly in boxes. Which is why it stings when the complexity gets flattened into a single tick mark. While the soul knows the universe runs on masculine and feminine, the human body knows how complicated, uncomfortable, and beautiful it is to live in the overlap.

At the heart of this human confusion is the ancient cosmic prank called duality. The tension between 'this' and 'that'—certainty and chaos. In every debate, both sides are right and both sides are wrong. That's the joke.

Life isn't about judgements or picking sides. It's about holding multiple truths without spontaneously combusting. Respecting that another person's truth can differ from yours, and that's okay.

Beyond human squabbles, consider the architecture of existence. On one hand, Matter: Particles, form, substance. On the other, Spirit: Energy, frequency, the intelligence that animates matter. Science calls it 'wave-particle duality'. Mystics call it Shiva and Shakti. Same phenomenon, different accent.

The universe began with one Big Bang, where pure energy condensed into matter. Galaxies, stars, planets, people: All sculpted from that first cosmic lovemaking. But the dance never ended. Energy collapses into particles when observed; particles dissolve back into energy when they die.

We are proof of it. Our body is matter. Our breath, spirit. Our cells vibrate with both solidity and emptiness. Ignore one side and you become either a soulless machine or a spaced-out mystic. Harmony comes when both are honoured.

Here's where yoga comes in—again. Among the 112 energy channels, or Nadis, that criss-cross the body, two stand out: *Ida*, which governs the left side, and *Pingala*, which governs the right. This is mirrored in the brain's hemispheres.

Ida Nadi is lunar, feminine, cooling. It snakes up the left side, linking to the right hemisphere. It is the house of creativity, emotion, and dreams.

Pingala Nadi is solar, masculine, heating. It climbs the right side, linking to the left hemisphere. This is the house of logic, action, planning, and doing.

In the centre sits *Sushumna* Nadi, the highway of spiritual awakening. When Ida and Pingala are balanced, energy flows through Sushumna. This is where the inner marriage—or union—happens. The inner masculine and feminine stop trying to dominate each other and finally dance together.

And that is the function of love—union. Not union with another person, but union within yourself. The other person is just the mirror, here to expose your split so you can integrate your own masculine with your feminine, your matter with your spirit.

That's why relationships feel like war zones. Your partner isn't 'being difficult'. They're poking every imbalance in your system. If your feminine is buried, they trigger your neediness until you reclaim it. If your masculine is frozen, they push your boundaries until you learn to hold them. They aren't here to complete you. They're here to expose you.

This is embodied in the deity *Ardhanarishvara*—half male, half female—a fusion of Shiva and Shakti. True liberation comes when we integrate our own polarity.

THE FINAL SOLO

For years, I thought I was fighting for equality, when in fact, I was just fighting within myself.

However, when the masculine and feminine energies inside stopped fighting, I stopped choosing sides—logic or feeling, action or rest, doing or being—I saw something fascinating: What looked like opposites were never separate at all.

What looked like 'two' was always just 'one' playing dress-up.

That's how life operates. It needs contrast to reveal itself. Without dark, there's no light. Without sorrow, joy has no flavour. Without inequality, there is no equality. Without chaos, peace has no meaning. The world loves a binary: God and Devil, Heaven and Earth, Matter and Energy, Left Wing and Right Wing, Coke and Sprite. But beneath the costume changes, there's only one current running the whole show.

Advaita Vedanta figured this out long before anyone could tweet about it. Advaita literally means 'not-two'. It's one of the boldest, simplest teachings in Indian philosophy—and it laughs at our obsession with categories. Male/Female. Good/Bad. Self/Other. Advaita shrugs: None of that's ultimately real. It's all Maya. A cosmic prank. Spiritual theatre to keep things interesting while consciousness plays hide-and-seek with itself.

At the heart of reality, there's only *Brahman*—pure consciousness, infinite and unchanging. Everything we think we are—this body, this name, these traumas, this curated personality—is just Brahman in disguise. Atman (our true self) and Brahman (ultimate reality) aren't two things. They're the same. Always have been.

One of Advaita's favourite metaphors nails it: Imagine you're walking at dusk and see a snake on the path. Suddenly, there's fear, panic, adrenaline. But look closer—it's just a rope. The snake never existed, but the reaction was real. That's Maya. We keep freaking out over illusions, mistaking the rope for the snake, forgetting to pause long enough to notice the truth underneath.

Duality works the same way. The battle between 'this' and 'that' only exists because we're peering through a fractured lens. When the lens clears, the fight disappears. No sides. No right. No wrong. No superior. No inferior. Just one.

Ancient India even tried to weave this truth into society with the *Varna* system—long before it calcified into caste. Varna literally means 'colour'—not of skin, but of energy, the hue of your inner wiring. There were four:

1. **Brahmins:** The seekers of knowledge, truth, and spirit. Think priests, teachers, and philosophers. Their role wasn't to dominate, but to preserve and transmit wisdom, guiding society towards higher understanding.

2. **Kshatriyas:** The protectors and warriors. Not just in battle, but in upholding justice, dharma, and societal order. Their strength was meant for protection, not conquest.

3. **Vaishyas:** The providers. Farmers, merchants, traders; those who created prosperity, handled resources, and ensured the community's well-being through stewardship of wealth and commerce.

4. **Shudras:** The caretakers and workers. The hands-on, practical force that kept society moving: Artisans, labourers, and service providers. They grounded the whole system through their contributions.

At its core, this wasn't about hierarchy. It was ecosystem thinking: The river isn't better than the mountain, the tree isn't superior to the wind. Different roles, equal value. People were guided to paths that matched their tendencies—knowledge, courage, generosity, or service.

But, of course, humans did what humans do best: We broke it. What was meant to harmonise became a hierarchy. Birth replaced aptitude, power replaced dharma, and oppression wore a sacred mask. Because if there's only one consciousness playing all the roles, any sense of superiority is just another snake on the path. Another illusion. Another distraction from the truth.

The journey was never about adding layers. It was always about peeling them away. About letting the illusion of separateness dissolve until there's nothing left but that quiet, spacious awareness where the need to be 'somebody' finally lets go.

SOLULU 6

Surrender to Insignificance

The world sells us a million ways to be somebody. Somebody successful. Somebody smart. Somebody desired. Somebody important. Life hands us a checklist and dares us to finish it: Degree, career, relationship, children, retirement plan, and a filtered funeral. Somewhere along the way, we mistake milestones for meaning.

But let's be honest—most of us aren't chasing purpose. We're chasing applause. We don't want freedom; we want validation. We want our existence stamped by job titles, wedding albums, blue ticks, or—at minimum—the algorithm. We want to prove we mattered. That someone looked at us and thought, 'Wow! What a Somebody.'

And there is no shame in that. If you still need to prove something, go ahead. Get the trophy, get that revenge, get married, have children, change your gender. Maybe your soul needs to be somebody before it remembers it was never anybody to begin with. That's part of the process.

Here is the twist: We don't just define ourselves by achievements—we define ourselves by our wounds. Anxiety becomes a personality. Trauma becomes a Tinder bio. And 'survivor'? That's just 'victim' with PR. You're not special for surviving life. Everyone's surviving life. The real work isn't branding your scars; it's outgrowing them.

Eventually, life will exhaust you. It will give you the promotion you thought would fix everything, the lover you thought would complete you, the body you thought would finally be worthy—and none of it will satisfy the ache. Here is where you either collapse under the weight of your own expectations or begin to gently let go.

The mystics knew this long before the philosophers and psychologists did. That's why Buddha walked away from his palace. Why Shams left Rumi. Why Jesus willingly died on the cross. Why the wise across ages and cultures kept repeating the same inconvenient truth: The self you're working so hard to become is not the real you. It's a costume stitched together to survive in a world terrified of nobodies.

You don't need to quit your job, shave your head, or cancel your LinkedIn Premium to get this. You just need to notice the itch beneath the striving. Why do you want that title, that partner, that award, that six-pack? Who are you really trying to impress? And do they even care?

When you become a nobody, I promise you, life will start flowing in ways you can't predict. Opportunities will come not because you chased them, but because you became light enough to receive them. Purpose will find you—not through striving, but through surrender. The right people will show up at the right time and the right paths will open. Not because you forced them, but because you finally stopped blocking them with your desperate need to belong, to be special, to be important.

The only way to make peace with that void you feel is to become the void: Shi-va.

Delulu 7

LIFE IS UNFAIR

'The universe is not punishing you or blessing you. The universe is responding to the vibration you are emitting.'

– Abraham Hicks

CHARGES FILED

There comes a point in every semi-conscious adult's life when they're punched in the gut and they scream, 'Life is so unfair.' Usually, it's when you realise that good behaviour doesn't protect you from bad outcomes, and life is not a vending machine that rewards kindness with cookies. Sometimes, the assholes win . . . a lot.

We live in a world where wars are orchestrated by men who wouldn't last a single day on a battlefield. Where the soft-hearted get chewed up, the loyal get cheated on, and the truthful get lied to. Where people who've done the inner work are still paying interest on someone else's karma, and those who clearly skipped the emotional syllabus are out there leading nations and running billion-dollar empires.

It doesn't make sense because it's not supposed to. The truth is that life isn't engineered to be fair. It's engineered to be revelatory.

Still, it's hard not to feel like you've been personally targeted by the cosmic HR department—especially if you're even remotely decent or emotionally aware. You start wondering if the idea of a loving God was just a PR stunt to sell church pews. Because what kind of 'Compassionate Creator' lets narcissists flourish while innocents get steamrolled?

But maybe the real question isn't why life is unfair. It's why we ever expected it to be.

We were conditioned from birth to believe in fairness. Be good, and good things will come. Follow the rules and you'll be rewarded. Pray hard, manifest harder, vibrate high enough, and surely God will swipe right on your dreams. But when that doesn't happen, the betrayal cuts deep. And when you see someone lie, cheat, manipulate, and still get exactly what they want, something inside you fractures.

Here's the glitch: Society doesn't run on compassion. It runs on fear.

A beggar asking gently is ignored. A robber demanding at knifepoint? Obeyed instantly. We don't yield to goodness; we yield to force. That's centuries of conditioning—fear God, fear government, fear the system, fear your parents. Fear anyone who has the power you think you don't. That's why we live in a world where kindness is strategic, compassion is performative, and morality is basically marketing.

And if that realisation makes you want to throw your phone in the ocean, sell your belongings, and go scream into a mountain, welcome. You're not broken—you're waking up. That grief you feel for the world is the illusion finally crumbling.

Oftentimes, when the illusion crumbles, it'll make you want to kill yourself. This is why even people with seemingly 'perfect' lives still want to jump off rooftops. It's because collapse always comes before clarity. And if you've ever been dragged into this dark, painful chapter of the syllabus, congratulations. You're not a victim—you're a candidate for liberation.

The secret is simple: Stop expecting fairness. Start searching for the truth.

SUMMONS SERVED

I spent my twenties expecting the universe to reward me for being a 'good person'. I treated decency like a loyalty programme: Be kind, work hard, speak the truth, and surely life would give me a decent ROI. Instead, I got heartbreak and burnout.

And then came the pandemic.

Queen Bee was locked down with her partner. I had the Mumbai flat to myself. But it wasn't 'freedom and healing'. It was 'burnout and beating'.

Our non-profit dealt with domestic and sexual violence, and the irony wasn't lost on us. While the world said, 'Stay home, stay safe,' we knew home was the least safe place for many. Violence surged behind closed doors. Suddenly, our mission felt more urgent than ever, and our workload tripled overnight.

In the middle of this societal unravelling, both my parents tested positive for COVID.

My father isn't just your average Indian uncle with opinions and high cholesterol. He clawed his way up from earning less than Rs 12,000 a month in 2000 to becoming one of Asia's top gastroenterologists. My mother had been his partner in every way—wife, administrator, emotional anchor, co-dreamer. Together, they poured their entire life savings into converting a crumbling four-storey building into a sleek hospital for digestive healthcare. Six years of back-breaking work, mortgaged properties, and one massive loan later, it was finally running smoothly . . . until it wasn't.

Three months into lockdown, the hospital couldn't pay rent. Turns out, when people are terrified of dying from a respiratory virus, gas and acidity lose their urgency. Their landlord, smelling profit in crisis, decided this was the perfect time to evict them and convert the place into a COVID hospital. He gave them a brutal ultimatum: 'Pay up or get out'.

My father, in his classic 'Fuck it, we'll rebuild' style, didn't blink. Even with half the loan unpaid, he decided to walk away. And, as poetic timing would have it, both he and my mother got COVID the same week we had to vacate the premises.

This left my sister and me to deal with the mess on our own during a nationwide lockdown and at the peak of Mumbai's monsoon season. To add to this, there were goons sent by the landlord, standing outside, circling the building, trying to intimidate us. We ignored them and kept going.

We contacted scrap dealers, negotiated rates we had no benchmark for, figured out how to dismantle medical equipment, load trucks, move things—all while navigating flooded roads, power cuts, staff that wouldn't show up, and a city shut down to everything except panic.

We stripped the building bare, sold what we could, hauled what we couldn't. My parents were in quarantine, completely consumed by their own health crisis. The life they had built was collapsing. But in a way, it felt like a blessing that they weren't there to witness it being torn down.

Because there was one part that even broke me.

On the first floor of the hospital stood a Devi temple my mother had built. At its centre was a *Bhairavi Yantra* consecrated by Sadhguru himself—a kind of energetic motherboard for divine feminine consciousness. My mother had cared for it every day with devotion. It had held space not just for her, but for hundreds of patients who walked in burdened and left lighter.

I powered through everything, but packing Devi amidst the rubble was the hardest. I remember wrapping her up piece by piece, hands shaking, trying not to cry. Yet even then, something steady filled the room—as though Devi was watching the collapse without fear, knowing something we didn't.

Real estate being what it is in Mumbai, there weren't many options. So, the temple came home with me—to the flat I shared with Queen Bee. That's when things in my life began to shift, and in our relationship, too.

Letting go of the hospital, though painful, turned out to be the best decision my parents could have made. My father's decades-long fight to prove his worth was finally over. And poetically, on the day they handed over the keys, the hospital was listed in the *Times Health Survey* as No. 1 in India for gastroenterology. Devi hadn't abandoned them. She had liberated them.

But back then, in the thick of it, nothing felt cosmic. It just felt like survival. Everyone at home was stressed, tensions were high, bills loomed, futures blurred. I was back to my daily hustle, my parents were dealing with the aftermath, my sister had returned to her world.

Despite all this, I didn't feel strong. I felt useless.

I was still in a job that paid me peanuts. I wasn't contributing financially to the family crisis. I wasn't fixing anything. Even though no one expected me to, I had internalised this warped pressure to become useful. Every time I felt the pinch of not earning what I could be earning, I accused Queen Bee of exploiting me, spiralling us back into our toxic loop.

There wasn't a single person I could truly collapse into—no one who could see what I was holding. And so, in true millennial fashion, I tried to fill the gaping hole in my chest the only way I knew how: With a pet.

Enter a cute grey Persian kitten. I named her Bilaroo—which just means 'cat' in Gujarati—because that's how emotionally fried I was. She didn't need a fancy name. She just needed to stay.

But guess what? Even she didn't.

Exhibit A: Loss

Bilaroo had become my tether to sanity. She scaled the balcony parapet like a mountaineer in training. I sealed every possible escape route with nets, cable ties, and borderline paranoia. Except one window—the one no one had touched in three years, until my mother visited and complained about a smell in the room.

On 9 July 2021, my parents dropped by for a rare visit. Bil had just turned one. I remember my father, a man infamous for his no-pets rule, picking her up and kissing her. This was the man who wouldn't let a dog sniff his shoes. In hindsight, it felt less like affection and more like a cosmic curtain call. At the time, I was too buried under deadlines to see it.

Close to 1 a.m., I was still stuck in Zoom meetings with Queen Bee when I realised I hadn't fed her. 'Bil, food!' I called out—the sacred incantation that never failed. Silence. The kind of silence that presses down on your chest like a bad omen. I searched frantically, heartbeat in free fall, until I remembered the window. Trembling, I leaned out. There she was—a small grey figure, motionless on the ground below.

I don't remember the exact sequence after that. My brain hit survival mode. Somehow, I made it downstairs. She lay in a pool of blood, a trickle from her nose. I collapsed beside her, sobbing, cradling her lifeless body. A stranger handed me a bedsheet to wrap her in. Their face is gone from memory, but that gesture remains carved into me.

The hours that followed blurred: Frantic calls, my parents arriving with an icebox, the decision to cremate her the next day. I sat in the car's back seat, grief-stricken, laptop open, working on the same PowerPoint I'd been making before she died—a project that, ironically, never went anywhere. That's how warped I was, unable to put down my hustle even in the face of death.

That night, grief came in waves—numbness one moment, tsunamis of 'what ifs' the next. Why did I open the window that hadn't been opened in years? Why did my parents—who almost never visited—come on that exact day? The more I replayed it, the more it felt orchestrated.

That week, my mother had to fly to Delhi. In my haze of grief, I decided to join her and take Bilaroo's ashes to the Ganges. As I released them at the confluence of the icy Mandakini and the muddy Alaknanda in Rudraprayag, two yellow butterflies appeared and hovered above the water where the ashes dissolved. And in that moment, I swear I heard something whisper: 'I'll be back.'

If that wasn't enough to trip me out, Rishikesh added its own twist. Sitting on a river beach, my hand brushed against something. I pulled it out—a perfect heart-shaped stone, the exact grey of Bilaroo's fur, roughly the same weight she'd been when I first held her. I knew then that this tragedy was no coincidence. It had to mean something.

One part of me was convinced she'd reincarnate. And so began a year-long kitten hunt. I scanned every shelter and street corner, waiting for her to show up and leap into my arms. I was offered several opportunities to adopt a kitten, but it never felt right. Nothing did. Eventually, I let go and told myself it was just grief with a spiritual filter slapped on.

Beneath all that, Bilaroo's death cracked something open in me. Strangers started showing up. Neighbours I'd never spoken to before checked in on me. That's when it hit me like lightning—I'd never had real friendships. Not the kind where people show up without needing anything. My whole life, I'd been the overachieving lone wolf, surrounded by acquaintances I needed for work but emotionally orphaned.

Losing Bilaroo didn't just break me. It exposed every fault line I'd wallpapered over—the isolation, the hustle addiction, the quiet despair I kept trying to bury under achievement.

Slowly, I began to rebuild. Worked less. Slept more. Spent time with family. Went on a few dates. And when 2022 arrived, I made a resolution: I needed a radical transformation. That's when I turned to something that had worked for me eleven years ago with Sankar—the twenty-one-day Sadhana. This time, though, instead of Devi, I did it for Shiva, leading up to Mahashivratri.

Yogic science tells us that Mahashivratri is the most potent night of the year for spiritual evolution. It's a time when the northern hemisphere tilts in such a way that the human spine, if kept erect, becomes an antenna for higher consciousness. So, the tradition began: Stay awake, sit upright, remain aware.

I did the whole twenty-one-day preparatory cleanse leading up to the night, and then some. I went one step further and shaved my head—for the second time. Not to be dramatic, though—I mean, I do have a flair for the cinematic —but I needed a visceral ritual.

There's this old gardening principle: When you trim a branch, the plant redirects its energy to that exact spot, accelerating new growth. In the same way, shaving the head is an energetic rerouting. You tell your system: I'm clearing the static. I'm ready for new wiring.

In many Indian traditions, we shave our heads when someone dies because hair holds memory. It's also a way of telling the universe: I release the past. I make space for the new.

And that's how I made space for the next chapter.

CROSS-EXAMINATION

I had asked the universe for something new, and—as always—it showed up with a little theatrical flair.

It started innocently: A bike ride at sunrise. My car was in service, so I borrowed my father's motorbike and cruised through my island like a heroine in a coming-of-age film. Heads turned, the wind was in my hair, and for a moment, I felt untouchable. The universe loves a setup before a punchline.

On my way back, a drunk auto-rickshaw driver came hurtling towards me. I swerved to avoid a head-on collision, but his bumper caught my foot. Five hairline fractures. No surgery, no screws or metal plates—just a walker as my new best friend. The universe had slowed me down. Queen Bee's deadlines lost their grip, and for the first time in years, I had space to sit with myself.

Meanwhile, the show Queen Bee had once conceptualised—the one optioned by an Academy Award-winning producer—finally came back to life. Thanks to a contact I'd introduced her to, it was pitched again and greenlit by a leading OTT platform. We were in business. Except 'we' is a slippery word.

Queen Bee made an executive call: Neither of us would direct or produce. With the NGO work in full swing, it would be too much, she said. I'd edit instead. Never mind that I hated editing. But given I also had no experience running a large-scale production, and was currently hobbling around like a retired gladiator, I went along with it.

The show itself was dark—literally and energetically. Based on her years of working with women in prisons, it was a gritty drama about power, patriarchy, and pain. And as if art and life had signed a secret pact, the energy on set mirrored its theme: Power games, humiliation, bruised egos.

Queen Bee came home every day fuming about being disrespected by the director and producer. I, meanwhile, was almost grateful my accident had spared me the battlefield.

However, during an initial script reading, I met Mister Mirage—an actor on our show. Tall, masculine, deep voice, eyes of a lost poet and soul of a monk. We bonded over Instagram stories filled with spirituality and romantic longing.

One day, while chatting, I mentioned I was sick and alone. He drove over an hour with food and medicine, tucked me into bed, kissed my forehead, and left without making it weird. No one had ever shown me that kind of tenderness before. I was done for. I confessed my feelings. He confessed he had a partner, thirteen years together. He'd fought the world and an ex-wife to be with her. Things were rocky physically, but emotionally entwined.

By now, sharing the people I loved was practically a rite of passage. I told him I was open to exploration. I wanted him. He wanted me. The chemistry was thick enough to stir with a fork. But we decided to wait—three months—before taking it physical. We wanted it to be conscious, deliberate, sacred. Not just bodies colliding but energies merging. Finally, I had a partner who wanted to explore Tantric sex not as foreplay but as a path to God.

Within the first month, strange things began to happen. He'd feel electric surges every time I touched him. Once, mid-embrace, he looked at me in shock and said he saw a blue light emanating from my heart centre. Moreover, we'd both tear up inexplicably in moments of deep eye contact. No one had ever 'seen' me like this before.

We planned our sexual rendezvous months in advance. Our birthdays were a week apart, so I booked a boutique homestay—soft lighting, herbal teas, incense thick enough to summon Shiva himself. But before our sacred weekend, there was Bangalore.

Sadhguru was consecrating the first Naga in over 800 years—a snake-shaped energy form, a once-in-a-lifetime event. Mister Mirage wanted to join. I booked the flights and reserved us a room in Nandi Hills for the night after. It was shaping up to be a powerful portal.

But the closer we got, the further he receded.

I had just started becoming aware of my patterns, and he was in awe of that self-awareness. As a result, my vulnerability became a performance. I'd confess my flaws with a kind of curated humility, hoping he'd be impressed by my emotional X-ray vision.

Soon, everything I shared with him in raw honesty began to get weaponised. Every time he got uncomfortable, he'd grow defensive and lob back one of my own confessions at me like a diagnosis.

I didn't like what was happening, so I started to call him out. And he didn't like the fact that I called him out, so we argued. Trigger, react, retreat, repeat, until, like a ghost I should've seen coming, he blocked me—just like Sankar had.

A few days before our scheduled departure to Bangalore for the Naga consecration, he reimbursed me for the flight and exited the stage without an encore.

By that point, tragedy had practically become my default setting. First the hospital, then Bilaroo, then the fractured foot—and now, a heartbreak thrown in for symmetry. It was as if the universe had decided to test how much irony one human could survive before levitating.

Turns out, this was just the beginning.

The Karma Dossier

When I first set foot on the 'spiritual path', no one gave me a disclaimer. I thought it meant I'd glow from within, radiate sandalwood, and walk around like the human version of chamomile tea. Maybe a few blessings, some abundance, the occasional upgrade to business class. Instead, I got ghosted. Again and again.

But here's the truth about spirituality: A real Guru isn't there to fix your back issues. He exists to take a sledgehammer to every psychological crutch you've ever built, rip off the emotional plasters you've lovingly collected since childhood, and force you to look at every unhealed wound, every delusion, every denial you've buried under 'good vibes only' posts.

The spiritual path isn't about escaping karma. It's about swallowing the entire karmic buffet raw, unseasoned, and in one sitting.

Let's decode what that actually means.

Karma isn't 'do good, get good; do bad, get slapped'. Karma literally means 'action'. Every thought, every word, every deed leaves a residue—a ripple. Not in a neat Newton's third law way, but in a 'congratulations, your next ten lifetimes just got complicated' kind of way.

To understand this, meet the karmic gang:

1. **Sanchita Karma:** Picture a Costco-sized warehouse stacked to the heavens with all your past karma from every life you've ever lived. Every thought, word, action, lie, heartbreak, betrayal, orgasm, panic attack, and thirst trap—every single moment since you were an amoeba—is filed away in that spiritual storage unit. Most of it just sits there, chilling in karmic deep freeze.
2. **Prarabdha Karma:** This is the preloaded slice of that stockpile you carry into this life. It's the karma that's been allocated for you to burn in this lifetime. It determines who you're born to, what body you inhabit, the baseline circumstances. This is what most people call 'fate'.
3. **Agami Karma:** These are the future IOUs you're generating as you go. Every choice, every intention, every swipe left or right—it's a karmic invoice waiting to be delivered.
4. **Kriyamani Karma:** The big one. The karma you're making right now, in this moment. It's the steering wheel of your destiny. It shapes your Agami, softens your Prarabdha, and can even chip away at your Sanchita—one conscious choice at a time.

Here's the design: Every time you react unconsciously, refuse forgiveness, cling to grudges, or manipulate out of fear, you're loading the karmic dishwasher with more dirty plates. And just like junk food, the bloating shows up later—in your body, in your relationships, in that same argument you've had for the fifty-eighth time.

So, how do you burn karma? Not by running from life but by digesting it. By staying present in discomfort instead of numbing it. By pausing before you lash out, noticing the wound behind the outburst, and choosing differently. Every pattern you break, every reaction you soften, lightens the karmic load.

Therapy can actually help with this. Through cultivating self-awareness, you can unpack your Prarabdha (the cards you've been dealt) and start driving your Kriyamani (your current response to those cards) with a little more maturity. But the moment you sign up with a Guru, you're essentially telling the universe: 'I don't want the starter pack. Give me the full karmic archive. Dump it all.'

And the universe, being the overachiever it is, complies.

With the Guru's grace, your Prarabdha gets shoved into fast-forward, and the doors to your Sanchita—the karmic warehouse that wasn't even supposed to hit you this lifetime—swing open. Suddenly, ten lifetimes' worth of drama comes crashing into your inbox at once.

This is why the lives of the devout look like demolition zones. This is also why 'good people' tend to suffer more. Friendships dissolve. Lovers ghost. Careers implode. Families fracture. Chronic illness, breakdowns, betrayals—they come not as punishment but as purification.

So why would anyone in their right mind sign up for this? Same reason people join a gym. It hurts, but the endgame is strength. Except this is a gym for your soul. And the prize isn't a six-pack—it's perception sharp enough to cut through illusion, and freedom from compulsive suffering.

Right now, your life probably looks like a 10,000-piece puzzle spilt across the floor with no box cover. Just fragments: Heartbreak, burnout, breakdowns. You keep staring at the chaos, wondering how it could possibly make sense.

But when you burn away the karma that's weighing your perception down, you start to realise that what broke you was also what built you. That the job loss, the heartbreak, the identity crisis, didn't happen *to* you—it happened *for* you.

Suddenly it dawns: *OMG! The universe is actually on my side!* There is no such thing as death or loss. There is only life—and profit.

And that's the beginning of the end of suffering.

PROCEEDINGS

After Mister Mirage pulled a Sankar-style vanishing act, I flew to Bangalore, heartbroken but weirdly calm. Not because I saw or understood the bigger picture—I didn't. But some part of me knew that the mess was part of the renovation.

Through a WhatsApp group, I'd connected with a fellow participant from Mumbai, Kapil, who offered me a carpool. The plan was to stop by my hotel and drop my luggage first, but in a rare bout of spiritual enthusiasm—or sheer laziness—we drove straight to the venue. I had enough emotional baggage to carry, so for a change, I decided to leave everything in the car: My suitcase, money, phone—everything except my yoga mat. *Ha-freaking-ha*!

The Bangalore centre was basically a muddy construction pit dressed up as a consecration ground. Fifteen thousand people crammed into a valley an hour and a half from civilisation, jostling like it was a BTS concert. I gave up on lunch after ninety minutes in the queue, then missed the gates closing for the seating area entirely. No matter. I found a spot by a giant LED screen, unrolled my mat, and settled down like a good little yogi.

As soon as I took my seat, the weather gods clocked in: Wind, check. Cold, check. Drizzle, check. I was wearing a thin cotton kurta, had no umbrella, and zero backup plan.

The moment Sadhguru walked on stage, the skies split open with a full-throttle, monsoon-style downpour. After four hours of relentless rain, my mat dissolved in the mud, my body cramped, my teeth rattled. I cried—part hunger, part cold, part bodyache from sitting cross-legged, part soul-level despair. 'Why did I sign up for this much discomfort?' I whimpered to the sky.

At 10 p.m., they gave us a break, and the rain paused like it was a participant, too. Apples were distributed. I managed to snag one. Miraculously, I found a crumpled 500-rupee note in my pocket and sprinted to a pop-up store to buy dry trousers. My small win was short-lived. Fifteen minutes into the next session, the rain returned, and my dry trousers were history.

Somewhere in the soggy chaos, Sadhguru mentioned that every participant had been given a copper snake at the entrance to deposit at the shrine—a ritual meant to extend one's lifespan after this karmic burn. Monks, he said, weren't given one because they'd chosen to accelerate their karma-clearing.

Guess who hadn't entered the seating area through the main gate and therefore hadn't received the copper snake? Apparently, the universe had quietly signed me up for the monk curriculum. *YOLO*, I thought grimly. *Let's burn the karmic house down.*

By 1:30 a.m., the programme ended. I peeled myself off the earth like a drenched gladiator, only to discover my carpool—along with my belongings—was gone. No phone, no wallet, no clothes, no clue. Volunteers tried to help, but all I knew was his first name: Kapil. In a crowd of fifteen thousand, that was like asking someone to find 'John in London'.

By 3:30 a.m., shivering and starved, I gave up. Everyone had left. I mustered every last bit of strength and courage I had and decided to walk 5 km to the highway and hitchhike. Just as I took my first step, headlights swept across the mud, and a stranger pulled up. He wasn't headed my way, but one look at me—hungry, muddy, freezing, on the brink of collapse—and he didn't hesitate. We got lost in the hills, his phone died, his charger didn't work, but somehow, against all odds, he delivered me to my hotel by 5 a.m.

I had no clothes, so I was banking on a hotel bathrobe. But no such luck. After explaining my situation to the hotel staff, they handed me a uniform, and I wore it like couture before collapsing into bed.

The next morning, reality came knocking. My phone, wallet, clothes, laptop—everything—still missing. I borrowed a staff member's phone and logged into Instagram, praying for a breadcrumb. After a few frantic messages, I learnt that Kapil had a flight to catch and had left my belongings with a monk at the venue. But now, I had to get back to the venue—an hour away.

Just then, in a resort that was practically empty, a man walked by with his wife and daughter. He looked vaguely like he belonged to the Isha tribe, so I asked. He did. I described my predicament. He smiled and said, 'Perfect. My wife was trying to avoid visiting Naga. Now she has no choice.' And just like that, he, too, drove me in the opposite direction of where they were headed.

That's when it landed like a warm, quiet truth: Even if you're stranded with nothing. Even if you're cold and alone and ankle-deep in spiritual sludge. Even if everyone you trusted has vanished. There is something—someone—that will show up for you.

And maybe, just maybe, that is grace.

THE WITNESS

After Naga, something cracked. I finally felt ready to sign up for *Samyama*—the Everest of Isha programmes. No registration fee, just an interview and two months of brutal preparation: Hours of daily practice, a 50 per cent raw vegan diet, no caffeine, no sugar, no intoxicants. Basically, none of the things that made life fun. Yet strangely, I was ready.

One day, amidst my prep-induced endorphin haze, I texted Sankar: 'I think you're finally out of my system'. And what happened after that, you already know. But here's the detail.

As soon as we were back together, the universe, with its twisted sense of humour, sent his wife to Japan to tend to her dying mother, leaving him alone for the first time in a decade. The timing was undeniable.

Meanwhile, Queen Bee, who had tolerated my crush on Mister Mirage, suddenly lost her composure over Sankar's return. The romantic birthday trip I had planned with Mirage? I invited Queen Bee instead. She flew in, fully aware she was the substitute, and made sure I knew how many plans she'd cancelled to be there for me.

It was the most cringeworthy birthday of my life. I spent half the time texting Sankar, while Queen Bee sat across from me, radiating silent fury. Naturally, guilt crept in, so I overcompensated with intimacy I didn't even want—the kind that leaves you feeling nauseous afterwards, wondering why your body has become a damage-control performance art piece.

And then, on the eve of my birthday, Sankar called at midnight. 'Ask me for anything today,' he said, 'and I promise I'll give it to you.'

Without thinking, I blurted out that I wanted a *Bhuta Shudhi Vivaha*—a sacred yogic union. I told him I didn't care about legalities or papers. I didn't even want him to leave his wife. I just wanted a ritual that would bind our energies the way our souls had always been bound. He promised he would make it happen.

I believed him enough to tattoo his name across my wrist —as though permanence could force his presence. To be fair, I wouldn't have if his name hadn't also meant Shiva. But the day I walked into the house with fresh ink on my skin, Queen Bee imploded. By then, we were already sleeping in separate rooms.

One night, she barged in mid-video call with Sankar while I was in a compromising position. That was the end of her illusion. Everything at work began to collapse, and honestly, I didn't care. Samyama was coming, and I poured everything into preparing for it.

Samyama was eight days of silence, intense yogic practice, and no escape. If Naga had stripped me of my fears, Samyama came to force me to let go. It was designed to open the warehouse of Sanchita Karma, to give me a gallery view of my physiological and psychological processes. And let me tell you—it delivered.

When it ended, Sankar was supposed to pick me up, like the old days. Except, he forgot. He was entertaining guests who knew his wife. He told me to *kill time* and take a cab to his place at night. By the time I got there, I was squatting in a roadside temple like a homeless prophet, waiting for him.

He eventually showed up, but there was no food, no tenderness—just empty vessels in the sink, a casual offer to pour me a drink, and the assumption that sex was the only form of communion we knew. He passed out. I sat awake, starving, replaying the irony: Eight days of silence, only to return to the deafening void of someone who couldn't even ask if I had eaten.

The next morning, he asked me to hide in the bedroom while his guests visited. Later, he disappeared with them for breakfast and returned just in time to make me late. No decency to pack me a meal, no time to stop for anything on the way, no attempt whatsoever at dignity. Food was never on Sankar's survival checklist—just sex and secrecy.

On the way to the airport, twelve years of quiet swallowing finally erupted. He looked genuinely shocked, as though he'd only just discovered I had vocal cords. He muttered apologies, thin and perfunctory, but at least they were words.

Mahashivratri was a week away. He knew how much it meant to me and wanted to make it right. He invited me to his tribal village for the festival—promised we'd share something outside the four walls of his bedroom. And so I went. Because hope, like karma, is a bitch.

When the day came, he did take me out—to a quiet spot by the Bhavani River while the rest of the village prepared. Venus and Mars were in conjunction, fireflies danced around us, and the sacred flame blazed on the mountaintop. For a moment, it felt cinematic, almost Disney. We kissed, and I almost believed it—maybe we were real.

But like all Sankar stories, the magic had a short shelf life. By 9 p.m., he'd passed out, leaving me in bed instead of at the temple or the village festival I'd come all this way for. No vigil. No ritual. No communion with Shiva. Just another night of broken promises.

The next morning, I was on my period—bleeding and raw—when he asked if we could *try it rough*. I said yes, out of sheer curiosity to see how unconscious he could get. He didn't check once if I was okay. I wasn't.

As soon as he finished, his phone rang. It was his wife. He leapt out of bed and whispered sweet nothings into the receiver for half an hour while I lay there like a discarded prop.

That's when something snapped. I pulled on my clothes, stormed downstairs, and let it all out in one volcanic eruption. To my surprise, he didn't run, gaslight, or silence me. He trembled and listened. He even admitted the damage and promised he'd try to do better, to repair what he'd broken.

By the time I returned to Mumbai, Queen Bee had morphed into a full-blown emotional parasite. The manipulations were no longer subtle; they were operatic. She weaponised every sacrifice, making me feel like I owed her my soul. And by the end of that month, I snapped.

It wasn't perfect with Sankar, but at least he was trying. And for the first time, I felt like I had something worth losing everything else for. I didn't care if the projects collapsed, if the organisation died, if Queen Bee failed in her mission, if I ended up broke, homeless, or jobless. None of it mattered. I had the love of my life. And that was enough to finally leave.

PRELIMINARY HEARING

The day I cut ties with the NGO, it felt less like a career move and more like an exorcism. Queen Bee's emotional tentacles had been coiled around my nervous system for so long that the moment I severed them, I could actually hear myself think. And in that rare silence, one thought strutted in like a drunk uncle at a wedding: *Call Ajay.*

Ajay had been hovering around the edges of my life since 2016, ever since we met at that twenty-one-day detox programme right before Queen Bee showed up. He ran a yoga school in Thailand, spoke like he'd swallowed a shaman, and had been pestering me to work together. I, of course, was too busy chasing romantic avalanches and crawling out of their debris to take him seriously. But now, stripped of illusions and income, I messaged him: 'Let's do it'.

I packed up my basics, left Mumbai, and drove to Mysore. For a month, Ajay and I brainstormed, vision-boarded, and built the skeleton of a wellness brand. It was wholesome. Except something didn't click. Ajay, being Ajay, diagnosed the problem.

'We haven't embodied the brand,' he said, like he was announcing a terminal illness.

His prescription? A nine-day water fast in Kerala.

Day three of the water fast—31 March 2023—Sankar inaugurated his new theatre on the exact patch of earth where, twelve years earlier, we'd once pitched a tent. What was once mud and starlight was now a Japanese fan-shaped amphitheatre. His wife had flown down from Japan. Instagram was littered with photos. Everyone was invited except me.

It ripped open every wound he had given me across twelve years, all at once. When I told him I was hurting, he didn't hold me. He deflected, defended, and blamed me. On the third day of a water fast, that's basically a kick to the gut. I cried until even the water I'd been sipping left my body. And then, in the eerie stillness after the storm, I heard it: *Move to Coimbatore.*

Not just move. The guidance was oddly specific—an airy 3BHK overlooking the Velliangiri mountains at sunset. It felt like God had slipped me a real-estate brochure.

When I told Sankar I was moving to Coimbatore, he reacted like I'd just announced I was building a house on his lawn. He accused me of trying to trap him, as though Coimbatore was an elaborate mousetrap I'd designed especially for him. I told him this wasn't about him. At least, not entirely. I had other reasons: Proximity to Isha, and the fact that the vision simply wouldn't let me go.

But before I could chase the vision, life detoured me. A friend of Ajay's needed someone to document a retreat in Rishikesh. It wasn't paid, but it came with a mountaintop Airbnb, bonfires, and Himalayan sunrises and sunsets. So, after that water fast, I parked my car—with all my belongings still inside—at Bangalore airport and flew north.

The retreat was hosted at an Airbnb run by a man named Yash. Long beard, longer hair, a strict yoga routine, and the kind of guy who regarded small talk before sunrise as a crime against humanity. Everyone called him *Babaji.*

I didn't bother approaching him. Until, one day, he started calling me *Captaan*—a nickname that stuck faster than the camera strap on my shoulder. He lingered, watching me film with the same quiet curiosity Sankar had twelve years earlier. I didn't think much of it at the time—my attention was still magnetised to Sankar's latest comeback tour. But remember this, because from then on, Yash sat in the background like a ticking time bomb.

When the retreat ended, I landed back in Bangalore at 2 a.m. and didn't even wait for sunrise. I drove straight to Coimbatore, chasing the vision like a breadcrumb trail. When I walked into the first apartment I'd shortlisted, there it was: Three bedrooms, airy and spacious, framed by the Velliangiri sunset—exactly as I'd been guided. Without effort or negotiation, it was mine.

Once this Sankar–Sadhguru–me equilateral triangle came into play, things began unravelling fast. Promises broke. Illusions crumbled. And the truth was simple: Sankar was never going to do the work.

On 17 June 2023—exactly twelve years after our tent night—we stood in the same place, at the same time, fully aware we were trapped in a karmic loop that needed to break. Neither of us knew how. So, we did what addicts do: Dabbled and repeated every pattern until, finally, I told his wife—and he ghosted me.

That's when my travels began.

During that phase, on a camping trip with some Isha folks—to Sankar's village, no less—I met a man named Chi. We clicked instantly, but of course, he was married, too. The pull was undeniable, but we agreed: No intimacy until he had spoken openly to his wife. It floored me that the suggestion came from him. I had waited twelve years for Sankar to come clean, and here, Chi did it in less than twelve days. That integrity was respectable.

Not long after, we were both invited to a full-moon ritual. Chi's wife was invited, too. When she heard I'd be there, the tension was palpable. I asked him if I should stay away. His reply was simple: 'Why should you not come?' And that's when it hit me—how deeply Sankar had silenced my existence.

Instead of avoidance, Chi chose transparency. He sat his wife down and spoke honestly. That night, the three of us shared dinner like functioning adults. For me, it was absurdly healing. After years of being treated like a dirty secret, I was finally treated like a human being.

Over the next year, Chi became a steady, grounding presence. He cooked with me, joined my evening walks, helped host guests, even sent me flowers and cake for my birthday. There was no drama. We could go days or weeks without talking, and nothing shifted.

That's when it struck me: My madness wasn't a personality defect. It was reserved specifically for Sankar. My madness was his medicine.

And then, like a cosmic punchline, I remembered the very first SMS Sankar had sent me twelve years earlier when I'd banged up my head and landed in hospital with a concussion: 'Sending you healing Chi.'

Holy shit! Healing Chi had been delivered—twelve years later.

CONTINUED HEARING

It had been two years since Bilaroo died. By then, my reincarnation fantasy had faded onto the same dusty shelf where I kept all my half-baked spiritual theories. Until one day, a friend in Coimbatore asked if I'd adopt two Persian cats. One grey floof looked exactly like Bil.

Given my travel schedule, I flatly declined. She adopted them instead. Four days later, she called back in a panic and begged me to take at least one. Reluctantly, I agreed to take the white floof because I didn't want to be reminded of Bil. But separating them felt cruel, so I took both. That's when the strangeness began.

The grey one mirrored Bil in uncanny ways: Same behaviour and body language, same eating habits, same morning routine. Within fifteen minutes of entering my home, he was shaking hands and playing fetch—tricks I had painstakingly taught Bil years earlier. Training a cat is difficult. Training a two-year-old one? Forget it. And yet, here he was.

Every time I looked into his eyes, the familiarity was electric. Even the timelines made sense: Bil had died in July 2021, and this cat had been born in November 2021.

That's when the penny dropped: Death and loss are illusions. When the attachment dissolves, the essence returns, wearing a new costume. Energy can neither be created nor destroyed; it transforms. That's not spiritual fluff—that's physics. It gave me a strange reassurance. If my hypothesis held, Sankar would return. And if he did not, perhaps the real work was learning that I did not need him to.

The more I worked on myself, the more life mirrored back the love I thought I had lost. Every promise Sankar ever made to me and never fulfilled, other people started fulfilling. My sister gifted me the phone he'd promised, my mother gave me a diamond ring he'd promised, a house guest cooked me the meals he'd promised, and someone else gave me the warmth he'd promised.

And just when I thought I was done chasing Sankar, my phone rang. It was Yash—from Rishikesh. Landlord drama had him spiralling. 'Captaan, I'm thinking of starting from scratch. Do you know a place in South India where I could set something up?'

Instantly, Sankar's jungle monstrosity flashed in my mind—the one he was struggling to maintain while his wife was still in Japan. He'd once floated the idea of finding help or turning it into an Airbnb. Yash had the skills. Sankar had the space. And maybe, just maybe, having someone as grounded as Yash around could stop him from completely self-destructing.

My saviour complex revved into fifth gear. I hadn't seen Sankar in six months, and I was blocked on all channels. I knew that if I showed up at his door, his first move would probably be to threaten to call the police—which, to be fair, would have been a reasonable reaction. This had 'obsessive stalker move' written all over it . . . But I leaned into my madness in full consciousness.

Predictably, when I landed at his door, his first words were: 'I'm calling the cops.'

I handed him my phone: 'Please do. Plenty of evidence to put you behind bars, not me.'

He froze. Then, like a schoolboy caught doodling indecencies in his notebook, he sat down. Within minutes, we were laughing at the absurdity of it all. I told him about Yash and proposed the collaboration. He dismissed me instantly, then invited me in for coffee instead.

Six months of separation collapsed into ten minutes of banter. I told him I was writing this book. He begged me not to expose him. I told him I needed to. He understood —and even apologised for all the harm he'd caused. Before we knew it, we were back in his bedroom.

This time it was different. He was tender, present, and almost reverent. Tears slid down my cheeks because I knew: This was the last time. Before leaving, I pulled a card from my Osho Zen Tarot deck. Out of seventy-nine cards, the one that surfaced was *Letting Go*. Even Sankar, who treated mysticism like spam mail, softened. We both knew it was over.

Soon after, Yash's crisis evaporated, and I realised the whole melodrama was a cosmic decoy—an excuse to deliver me back to Sankar for one last, clean goodbye.

Three months later, Mahashivratri rolled around with another detour. It had been exactly a year since Sankar and I had last marked the festival together. This year, I was invited to a wedding in Triyuginarayan, a Himalayan village I hadn't even known existed. Turns out, it was the exact site where Shiva married Parvati on the night of Mahashivratri.

I booked my ticket and told Yash. We roped in another retreat alumnus for mountain downtime after the wedding. However, two days before the big day, the wedding was called off. By then, my bags were already packed and my plans with Yash were set. That's when I realised the wedding was never the point. Mahashivratri in Triyuginarayan was.

After a wild solo pilgrimage that left me battered, I half-joking, half-aching, texted Yash: 'I expect to be treated like a princess.' A line Sankar had once promised and never delivered. Yash didn't step up. But the other young man I was roomed with did. He was the kind of person who'd make space for you without being asked.

One morning, I joined him in his practices while Yash quietly did his own behind us. Out of nowhere, tears poured out of me with a reverence I'd never felt before. Could it be this man evoking these feelings? Surely not Yash. Yash was too cold, too armoured—the kind of guy who wouldn't even sling an arm around you for a photo.

Out of curiosity, I leaned into intimacy with the roommate one night. It felt wrong, and I aborted the mission immediately.

Meanwhile, Yash and I had one of those late-night talks. He dismissed Sadhguru as too flashy and praised his own obscure guru in Haridwar. It was the exact same gripe Sankar had. I didn't bother arguing. He also mentioned that his landlord saga was still dragging on and floated the idea of collaborating with me on an Airbnb in South India.

It aligned with what I wanted to do, too. So, when I reached home, I contacted real estate agents and made moves. Every time I asked him to fly down, he always had an excuse. Eventually, I lost steam, closed the chat, and let my adventures drift elsewhere.

Final Verdict

By the end of that year, I was practically unshakeable. I could watch life unravel without flinching, turn people's projections into compost, and stay calm in any storm.

My obsession with Sankar had dulled, but the sting of never being able to attend his shows in public still lingered. So, when I learnt he was staging a new production at his amphitheatre in the jungle, I felt the pull. Maybe if I went, I could cut the cord. Or maybe I'd just tangle it tighter. I didn't know. So, I asked the universe to decide for me.

Three days before the play, Yash called out of the blue: 'Captaan, I'm in Coimbatore.' After nine months of delays, he'd finally made it—arriving with a broken shoulder and a German woman. I invited them over. His long hair was gone, most of the beard, too. He looked less mystic, more man. They shared a room in my house, but the night before Sankar's show, she left for a retreat. Yash stayed.

I was shocked, honestly. I'd never seen him remotely close to a woman. Curious, I asked. He said nothing had happened . . . yet. He'd been celibate for five years and wouldn't break that streak unless he was sure. But from what I saw, the German seemed pretty sure.

That night, for the first time, Yash and I actually spoke. I unloaded my whole Sankar saga—twelve years of madness, heartbreak, obsession—and he listened. Not like men usually do, nodding half-distracted. He listened with full presence. No interruptions, no distractions, just holding space. It felt disarming. Sacred, even.

I confessed that I'd asked the universe for a sign about whether I should go to Sankar's play, and that I knew the universe had sent him to help me navigate this decision. He told me not to overthink it and that the answer would come.

He was right. The next morning, I woke up with Sadhguru's words echoing in my head: 'If you love someone, you should do what they want, not what you want.' Sankar didn't want me at his shows. He never had. So, the answer was simple. I wasn't going.

That day, I spent my time with Yash instead. Sharing space with him was harmonious in a way I'd never experienced with another human before. And when we chanted together in my temple space, our breath fell into rhythm as if it came from the same source.

The next day was Vasant Panchami—the day of Saraswati, Goddess of wisdom and new beginnings. I woke to find him doing his practices in my living room. Suddenly, the same reverence I'd felt in Rishikesh during Mahashivratri returned. Tears streamed down my face uncontrollably. I realised it had always been Yash.

Wailing, I went to his room and blurted, 'You're a gift from Saraswati. I don't know if this is love or what, but it is deep respect, and I feel like touching your feet.'

He smiled softly. 'Goddesses don't touch our feet. We touch theirs. The respect is mutual.'

Let me be clear: I have never wanted to touch anyone's feet in my life. My instinct around men has always leaned more towards slapping them. Traditionally, in India, wives touch their husbands' feet. I'd always barfed at that patriarchal nonsense. But for a moment, I couldn't help but wonder if there was some spiritual significance to the gesture.

It struck me then: All the promises Sankar had made but never fulfilled were being completed, one by one, through others. And perhaps the last—the *Bhuta Shuddhi Vivaha*, the yogic marriage I had once asked him for—was now circling back through Yash. It was too soon to conclude anything, so I told myself to stop hallucinating.

That evening, we went to Isha. Sankar had always resisted going inside. He once told me he would visit one day, but only when he truly felt ready—not out of pressure or obligation. It was one of those promises that lingered in the air, half-made, half-meant.

Yash, too, had avoided visiting Isha for two years, using the same line about 'not being ready'. But this time, he came willingly. Not only that, he participated in everything with a quiet reverence that felt as though Sankar's unfinished promise had finally found its way through Yash's feet.

That evening, we went to the Devi temple for a ritual. I had to submit his birth details. However, when I saw them, my stomach dropped. His sun and star were identical to Sankar's.

I could begin to see what was unfolding, but I was still in denial.

Later that night, I offered to apply herbal oil to his injured shoulder. He sat on the floor, back to me; I sat on the couch. The moment I touched him, time stilled. Without thinking, I leaned forward and hugged him from behind. He clasped my hand to his chest, and we stayed like that, breathing together—an hour dissolving into silence.

The stillness took me back to the first time I was intimate with Sankar in Pondicherry.

Yash left the next day. And after he did, the strangest thing happened: All the emotional files I'd stored in my 'Sankar' folder transferred, wholesale, into a new one labelled 'Yash'. The memory of a man I had struggled with for over a decade was overwritten overnight.

My hypothesis was right all along: Sankar was back. Same file, new body.

Energy transformed, not destroyed.

CASE DISMISSED

Karmic patterns aren't random mood swings from the universe. They're more like cosmic reruns—the same script, slightly different cast. You think you've moved on, grown wiser, left the ex, changed cities, changed wardrobes, maybe even done therapy. And then life smirks and says, 'Let's see how you do with the sequel.'

Every twelve years, the Sun completes its orbit, and you get re-enrolled in the same karmic classroom. Maybe the question paper is tougher this time, but the syllabus hasn't changed.

These cycles come in intervals of twelve, six, three, and one-and-a-half years (and months)—like celestial reminders. The ancients didn't pull these numbers out of thin air. That's why the Kumbh Mela, the world's largest spiritual gathering, happens every twelve years. The Ardha Kumbh, every six.

Each cycle is basically the universe's way of checking your progress report. 'Still chasing unavailable men? Still people-pleasing? Still pretending your trauma's a personality trait?' Tick, tick, tick.

Now here's a critical one: The thirty-two-to-thirty-three age window is a spiritual checkpoint. By then, you've gathered enough drama, heartbreak, and self-help books to fill a lifetime. At this point, the universe politely asks, 'So, evolve or repeat?'

Most people miss the memo. They hit thirty-two and start doubling down on delusion—new car, new spouse, same patterns. By forty, they're bloated with regret and trapped in marriages, jobs, and ideologies they don't even remember signing up for.

But for a few people—the ones who are paying attention—thirty-three becomes the jailbreak. The moment you realise freedom isn't about leaving your job or your partner; it's about leaving the loop.

When Sankar was thirty-two, the universe gave him that exact chance. I entered his life as the jailbreak. All he had to do was stop lying to himself, stop pretending, and choose truth over convenience. But fear dresses up as logic, and logic always sounds convincing. So, he stayed in the loop.

Twelve years later, it was my turn.

I hit thirty-two and saw the same pattern unfold—only this time, I wasn't in his orbit; I was in his position. The day I finally raised my voice, the loop cracked, and I was ready to step out of the Matrix. He wasn't. He clung to his delusions like a life raft, and, in the end, we drifted out of each other's frequency.

That's what yogic texts call Samsara and *Sannyasa*. Samsara is the karmic treadmill—same emotions, different storylines. Sannyasa isn't about renouncing life or shaving your head; it's about renouncing the repetition. You can be a monk and still be in Samsara, or you can be a householder and be totally free. Liberation is a state of mind.

Now, if you've missed your thirty-three window, don't panic. The universe is patient. It comes back around—forty-seven for the feminine energy, forty-two for the masculine. And if you miss that, too, sixty is the final tap on the shoulder: 'This time, really pay attention.'

My parents, bless their generational lag, hit that checkpoint right on schedule. The year before they turned sixty, the perfect marriage they'd curated for thirty-four years cracked. On my father's birthday trip, they met a woman their age and clicked instantly; so much so that she referred to my mother as *Ida* and my father as *Pingala*, the left and right energy channels.

A few months later, my mother discovered exchanges between this woman and my father that hinted at a deep emotional intimacy he had kept hidden. Cue the karmic fireworks at home.

While I was processing my own betrayal saga with Sankar, my mother was living hers. Watching her rage, grieve, and finally soften was like getting a 3D simulation of everything I'd put Sankar's wife through. For the first time, I had an inside view of what she might have felt—minus the empathy filters I'd conveniently kept in place.

At sixty, my parents began peeling away layers they didn't even know they'd been carrying, unlearning ideas about love, marriage, and themselves. Late awakening is still awakening, and watching them step into that light has been unexpectedly beautiful.

That's the thing about karma. It doesn't stop at individuals—it runs through bloodlines. Patterns pass from parent to child, like vintage jewellery, except instead of diamonds, it's abandonment issues and denial complexes.

But when you finally see the pattern, really see it, you stop playing victim. You start playing witness. You realise these aren't punishments; they're invitations to stop repeating and start remembering.

You stop asking if life is fair. You already know it is.

SOLULU 7

Assume All Responsibility

Existence, in all its chaotic brilliance, is absurdly fair. It just has zero interest in keeping you comfortable. It only wants you to grow. Life isn't punishing or rewarding you—it's upgrading your software, one meltdown at a time.

Of course, from the human vantage point, it feels like a huge scam. But zoom out, and you'll start to notice the symmetry in the madness. All that shit in your life was fertiliser. Pain has a strange way of composting into wisdom—and that growth begins when you take full responsibility.

Because the moment you say, 'It's not my fault,' you hand your power to whoever you've decided to blame—your ex, your parents, your guru, the economy, the planets, the system, the government, the media, the devil, the Illuminati, the cabal, Big Pharma, or your neighbour's evil eye. None of them is running your life. You are.

It starts with accepting that you are not a victim of life, but a student of life.

Everyone's in the same karmic classroom, working through their own karma, wounds, and insecurities. Often, your pain is of your own making. And sometimes, your pain is just their unfinished homework landing on your desk. But even that is an invitation—not to suffer, but to master compassion and boundaries in equal measure.

True responsibility isn't about self-blame either. Your mental health diagnoses, anxiety, depression, and trauma are not a hall pass for bad behaviour. Everyone's mentally unstable to varying degrees. Healing begins the moment you stop glorifying the wound and start taking responsibility for your recovery—and for showing up responsibly.

And that's where most people trip—because accountability feels heavier than blame. Responsibility requires you to acknowledge your role. It means dropping all the excuses, blaming nobody, apologising when you are wrong, and sometimes even when you are not. It means recognising that you have a choice: To heal the world by being compassionate, or to add more violence and pain to an already fractured one.

That's what being *response-able* really means—the ability to respond, not react.

We've been sold the lie that less responsibility equals more freedom. So, we avoid it and shift the blame. But the opposite is true. The more responsibility you take, the freer you become. Because when there's no one left to blame, there's no one left to control you.

Real healing isn't about avoiding red flags, running from the mirrors life sends you, building taller walls, or declaring, 'I'll never let that happen again.' That's not self-love; that's avoidance. True healing begins when you can trust life—allow situations to unfold knowing you may be hurt in the end, stand in the wreckage, look the pain straight in the eye, and ask: 'Alright, what are you here to teach me?'

Delulu 8

I WILL CHANGE THE WORLD

'Be the change

you want to see in the world.'

– Mahatma Gandhi

The Saviour Complex

When we're young, we all think we're here to fix something: The planet, our parents, the patriarchy. Some want to build schools in villages; others just want their ex to admit they were wrong. Either way, the fantasy's the same—we're the chosen ones.

So, when I joined Queen Bee's non-profit, I thought I was joining the revolution. I wore my purpose like a halo, blissfully unaware that halos, when worn too tightly, cut off circulation to the brain. I believed the vision, the mission, the tagline, and the funding deck. I believed that if we just worked hard enough, cared deeply enough, and used all the right buzzwords, humanity could be saved.

But here's the thing nobody tells you about 'saving the world': The world is not a damsel in distress waiting for you to show up with a grant proposal and CSR funds. It's a 4.5-billion-year-old hot mess that has survived ice ages, asteroids, and multiple Kardashians. It doesn't need saving. You do.

It took me a while to see that. At first, I blamed the usual suspects for things not working out: Lack of funding, bureaucratic red tape, lazy staff, bad luck. But eventually, the cracks widened and the truth spilled through—the problem wasn't the world. The problem was us.

Distance has a way of turning drama into data. When I finally stepped back, all those years at the NGO clicked into focus. We weren't empowering students to be responsible; we were teaching them the art of outsourcing responsibility by blaming sharper, shaming louder, and calling it justice. All our social justice crusades were just self-importance masquerading as compassion.

That's when I realised why the social sector lived in a perpetual state of lack and exhaustion. It is because it is feeding the most sophisticated beast of all: The righteous ego. Our NGO wasn't a temple of service—it was a theatre of virtue, with Queen Bee as the writer and director. And me, as the assistant director.

When I decided to leave, I did the unthinkable: I wrote a resignation email. Not a clean 'thanks for the memories' exit, but a full-blown confessional monologue. I laid out, point by point, every place I had manipulated in the name of the mission, every employee

I had exploited, every boundary I had bulldozed in the name of impact, every time I had weaponised ideals to control. Then I hit cc: All—staff, board, interns, even former employees.

I expected crucifixion. What I felt instead was baptism.

When Queen Bee finally got the 'emotional accountability' she'd demanded from me all along, she combusted. Within an hour, my server access vanished. Group channels disappeared. I was digitally exorcised—erased from the collective like a scandalous footnote. Given that I had publicly pled guilty, she now also had a scapegoat to pin all the dysfunction in the organisation on.

But strangely, I didn't care, because I no longer had any use for my reputation. For the first time, I wasn't trying to protect my mask. I just wanted the truth to breathe. I thought I'd outsmarted my ego. But, in true diva fashion, it staged a comeback tour. The moment I was cut off, I found myself trying to save everyone—from her and from the organisation.

It took a few days—and a few humbling conversations—for the storm to settle. Only then could I see the full picture with clarity. I'll be honest: I did give her a hard time. I thought I was the whistleblower of truth, but my ego was really just panicking—trying to prove I was better. Holier, wiser, righter.

Once the flames died, something quieter emerged—an unsexy but sobering insight: My 'altruism' was just another performance. I hadn't been trying to save the world from sexual violence; I hadn't even been trying to save people from Queen Bee. I'd been trying to save myself—from irrelevance, doubt, and the horror that maybe my existence didn't matter as much as I wanted it to.

The recognition left me itching with shame. But eventually, it softened into something else—the first honest crack in my self-awareness. Somewhere between signing up to change the world and pressing send on that email, my halo slipped and shattered.

And in its place, something humbler emerged: The realisation that maybe the only world I'm meant to save is the one between my own ears.

CODEPENDENCY COUNSELLING

I thought my saviour complex had died when I left the NGO, but it simply reincarnated with Sankar. Then, when Sankar left me, I naturally turned to the next available candidates—my parents.

As a child, I thought I'd won the parental lottery. My mother was the patron saint of sacrifice—the woman who gave up her dreams to build my father's. And my father, charming and ambitious, was the textbook narcissist. Yet, compared with most other families, we looked like an advert for emotional stability.

Then I grew up. Which apparently meant developing the nerve to challenge my father's opinions. When he trash-talked Queen Bee, I defended her. The day he called me a failure, I reminded him how he had to shut down his hospital. That particular jab landed so hard that he broke down sobbing and told me to get out of the house.

Any normal child might have stormed out, but I planted myself on the couch like Gandhi in yoga pants. 'This is my house, too,' I said. 'If you didn't want me, why did you bring me into the world?' He had no rebuttal. He sulked for a few hours, then grew tired of his own silent protest and resumed scheduled programming.

When I quit my job and officially became the family's 'unemployed failure', I had no choice but to ask him for money. There was judgement, of course—a few months of it, sprinkled with passive-aggressive taunts—until my parents came to visit me in Coimbatore. They were shocked to see my evolution.

My mother did something unprecedented: She bowed and touched my feet. My dad followed suit with words of reassurance. 'You carry on doing whatever you're doing,' he said. 'It's a privilege to work on oneself—a privilege I did not have. If you need money, I am here.'

Suddenly, I was being paid to simply exist. My ego couldn't accept that. So, with my track record in extramarital drama, I slid into the role of family crisis manager as if it were my job profile. I ended up playing my parents' marriage counsellor to feed my own self-worth.

I could appreciate that my dad was experiencing a sweet, harmless emotion like love. He wasn't burning the house down, and he had no intention of abandoning his family. He was just sharing poetry and love songs with another woman. I knew he loved my mother, too. But the lying and hiding? That's where I lost patience.

My mother naturally felt betrayed. She had given everything to this family, and emotional infidelity was the last thing she expected. Yet she kept insisting that her real wound was not so much the other woman—but the secrecy. My dad's defence was that telling her the truth usually ended with a dramatic outburst, so he avoided it altogether.

Thus began the loop: Trigger, react, repeat. There was no hero or villain here, just two people scratching each other's emotional mosquito bites raw.

And then there was my own inability to lie. If one parent confided something and the other interrogated me, I blurted it out. Cue chaos. One minute they were fighting, the next they were making tea for each other.

This earned me the family nickname *Narada Muni*—the divine mischief-maker of Hindu mythology who roamed the realms spreading spiritual wisdom . . . and occasionally, spectacular gossip. He did it to get people to confront their illusions and issues. My role, throughout my life it seemed, was to drop truth bombs in the middle of people's emotional minefield and watch the show.

Oddly enough, it worked. We started having raw, unfiltered conversations about things that had festered for decades—old resentments, unmet needs, even their sex life. No topic was off-limits. It was deeply uncomfortable but also liberating. For the first time, our family wasn't performing love; we were learning it.

Years earlier, for their twenty-fifth wedding anniversary, my parents had remarried at the Devi temple. Sadhguru had popped by to bless them personally. Society teaches us that 'blessing' means predictable peace, and that's what they had expected. But I saw it differently. This was the blessing. He had stirred the soil so that something real could grow.

I am extremely proud of my parents because they got the memo. Despite their compulsions, each of them chose to respond to situations with responsibility and grace. Over the next few months, my mother began travelling more, attending yoga retreats, and creating space between them. It was the medicine they both needed. They had been co-dependent for too long. Now, they were finally learning to breathe on their own.

My mother had always dreamed of opening a café in the mountains—something soulful, simple, and hers. My father was on board, ready to fund it and cheer her on. It felt like the beginning of a new chapter for both of them.

But before any of that could happen, life—being the messy editor that it is—dropped a plot twist. My grandfather in Singapore fell ill. My mother flew down, and with that flight, another layer of intergenerational healing began to unravel.

ANCESTRAL UNTANGLING

I'd always been close to my grandfather because I'd lived with him while I was at university.

My grandmother had died of heart failure when I was six months old, leaving him to preside over the house with that evil house help who treated us like chew toys when we were children. After twenty-eight years of service, she finally retired—only to be replaced by a woman whose life was a carbon copy of my mother's: Same marital drama, same martyr complex. The universe really doesn't waste a good mirror.

My relationship with my mum's side of the family was pretty much non-existent. Her elder brother had married a Chinese woman, the younger a Filipino, so we had cousins sprinkled across the family tree like exotic garnishes. Every attempt to get closer was derailed because nobody had the time or inclination. The underlying cause, however, was mostly religion. My mum had outgrown her Christian upbringing, but her brothers clung to theirs like toddlers clutching a security blanket.

The younger one was volatile—loving one moment, explosive the next. My mother, armed with her own saviour complex, kept trying to fix him, and every attempt ended in a fight. The elder brother was more polished but condescending. His intelligence had built him a pedestal so tall he couldn't meet anyone at eye level. My mother spent her entire life trying to earn his respect, and he spent his trying to prove she hadn't.

By the time my grandfather was hospitalised at ninety-one, the three siblings were locked in an icy stalemate. My mother camped at the hospital, chanting and staging her Hindu rituals like an exorcism, while her Christian brothers twitched in disapproval. Meanwhile, my father had been promoted from 'marital sparring partner' to 'full-time emotional support animal'.

I arrived in the middle of all this like a firefighter walking into a petrol station on fire. A dysfunctional family and a dying grandfather? My saviour complex was practically purring.

Grandpa was in rough shape. He couldn't eat, couldn't drink, barely spoke. I took the night shifts to give my mother a break. His dementia came in waves—tragic one moment, hilarious the next. In his lucid spells, he whispered that he was only hanging on because he didn't want to die while his family was still fractured. He wanted to go home, to the house where my grandmother had passed.

By day three of my arrival, he was sipping Milo and eating Mysurpa I'd brought from Coimbatore. My spiritual ego swelled like a helium balloon. Clearly, I was the miracle worker. So, I doubled down—counselling the siblings, mediating conversations, auditioning for Family Therapist of the Year.

One night, when I was alone with him, he became fixated on speaking to someone named Michelle. I had never heard that name before. On the bus ride to the hospital the next evening, I casually asked the househelp. She hesitated, then confessed: Michelle was an elderly Chinese woman who used to call the landline. Talking to her made him light up, until one day he told her to stop. She had no idea why.

The bus rattled on, but something in me stilled. I knew, without logic and without proof, that my uncle and Chinese aunt would be at the hospital that evening. They rarely showed up together, never on schedule. But I could already picture the scene.

Sure enough, when I walked in, there they were—exactly as I had envisioned it.

I laughed at the cosmic choreography. Here was a man who had spent years quietly judging his Chinese daughter-in-law, now haunted at the end, possibly by his own Chinese beloved. The universe does not miss a chance to write a tidy moral.

I told my uncle what I'd realised. He looked at me like I was peddling a conspiracy theory, denied Michelle's existence, and insisted my grandfather had never had a problem with his wife. Which was rich, considering I'd lived with Grandpa during university and heard his complaints more times than I could count.

The tragedy was glaring. Because of secrets, shame, denial, and the great family skill of avoiding uncomfortable truths, Michelle would never see him, and he would never hear her again. That thought sat in my chest like a stone.

That's when another truth started scratching at me—I was keeping a secret, too.

My father's 'lady friend' had made a set of Diwali lamps and wanted to gift them to my parents. My father, terrified of triggering my mother, asked me to accept the gift instead. I agreed, partly because I respected his effort to handle her affection with grace, partly because it was a dignity that Sankar had never afforded me.

After the Michelle revelation, I was done protecting anyone's illusions. I took my mother aside to the hospital's waiting lounge and told her everything.

She erupted.

Betrayal from her husband was one thing; betrayal from me was another. She stormed out of the hospital, leaving me behind for night duty—sitting in the fluorescent silence, wondering if truth always had to come at such a cost.

The Doorway of Death

That night, around 3 a.m., I stepped out of the hospital for air. Beirut was being bombed, and I saw Ziad's daughter post about it online. I messaged to ask if they were safe. She replied: 'There's no easy way to say this, but Dad died of a heart attack.'

I didn't feel pain or shock. Instead, I laughed out loud because I immediately saw the design. Exactly a month earlier, while visiting Isha, I had been struck by the intuition that Ziad wasn't okay. I'd texted him, after years, out of the blue: 'Don't panic. Life is happening for you, not to you.'

The lesson was glaring. I could not save my mother from feeling betrayed, I could not save my uncles from their egos, I could not save my grandfather from his suffering, or even Ziad from death. All I could do was stop pretending that I could.

The next morning, I picked up breakfast and went home to find my mother still starring in her one-woman tragedy about betrayal, as if grief were a competition she intended to win. Despite knowing that I had lost someone very dear to me, she continued to hog the limelight.

Suddenly, I realised we were standing in the exact spot where she'd once threatened to jump out of the window when I was six years old, stealing my crisis to stage her own.

For the first time in my life, I felt a rage that wasn't hot and reckless but cool and deliberate. It didn't yank me into a compulsive reaction; it invited me into a conscious act. I picked up a glass plate, locked eyes with her, inhaled deeply, and in one smooth motion, smashed the plate on the floor.

The crash was surgical—a clean explosion of sound, followed by a thousand tiny splinters scattering across the house. I then sat down and glared at her while she swept up the mess. The message was clear: This is what you've done with your emotions your entire life. Shattered them into sharp little pieces and handed them to other people to clean up.

That's when I finally understood the *Mahabharata*. It wasn't a senseless war; it was truth in action. Dharma, I realised, isn't polite. It doesn't always chant and sit cross-legged. Sometimes, it smashes plates.

Later that night, I meditated and reached for Ziad. He appeared—calm, matter-of-fact, and asked for the *Kalabhairava Karma*, a yogic ritual that releases the dead from the living. It must be done within forty-eight days, with a piece of the departed's clothing.

I thought I had nothing of his until an image of a green sweatshirt he'd left with me twelve years ago flashed before me. I called my parents' house-help in Mumbai. It was still there, folded neatly at the back of a cupboard—like a seed waiting for rain.

A part of Ziad had known that his Lebanese family would never perform the ritual, so he left it to me. That was our contract: not romance or comfort, but completion.

Ram Dass once said, 'We're all just walking each other home.' And I finally understood. Every person you meet is a fellow traveller—some stay for years, some for a single stop. Love isn't about forever; it's about walking someone as far as you can and then letting them go.

By then, my work in Singapore was done, too. We had managed to bring my grandfather home. He was still dying, but he had gone from not being able to sip water to chugging his favourite 100 Plus. He was where he wanted to be: his own bed, familiar walls, and the ghost of my grandmother somewhere in the rafters.

The day I left, he kept asking when I was flying out. He even called to check I'd landed safely. The man who'd forgotten my name that month suddenly remembered every detail. It was oddly tender.

The morning after I reached Coimbatore, I went straight to Isha for Ziad's ritual. As I sat there, I held my grandfather in my mind, asking the cosmic customs officer to please stamp his exit visa and let him pass without baggage.

Minutes after the ritual ended, my phone buzzed with a message from my mother. My grandfather had passed away peacefully. That's when I realised it wasn't the family feud that kept him tethered to suffering. He was waiting for me to learn my lesson. The realisation was humbling.

As cosmic choreography would have it, the funeral was planned for the next day, which also happened to be my paternal grandmother's birthday.

Just like that, birth and death lined up like two sides of the same coin, daring me not to see the design. One soul left, another celebrated—the universe's unsubtle way of reminding me that endings and beginnings are never separate events, just different points on the same circle.

THE MECHANICS OF LIFE

If you haven't noticed, life has a thing for reruns. Planets orbit, tides return, moods swing, and even the stock market behaves like toddlers on a sugar high. From galaxies spiralling above to the rise and fall of your own breath, everything runs on loops.

When Bilaroo reincarnated and Sankar re-entered my life as Yash, I finally stopped calling it a coincidence. Clearly, the universe runs a sophisticated recycling programme.

And as it turns out, science agrees. The Law of Information Conservation says that nothing is ever truly lost—not energy, not matter, not even memory. Every thought, emotion, and heartbreak you've ever had leaves an imprint on the quantum field. Consciousness is like a frequency broadcast through the body; when the body drops, the signal doesn't vanish. It simply tunes into another receiver.

Even biology hums the same tune. Every cell in your body carries memories you didn't personally live. Biologist Rupert Sheldrake called this 'morphic resonance'— the idea that memory isn't stored in the brain but in invisible fields connecting all living things. It's how birds migrate without maps and how a six-year-old suddenly starts playing Mozart. The mind forgets. The field does not.

Now, the fact that your mind remembers none of this is actually mercy. Imagine carrying lifetimes of heartbreaks, rejections, betrayals, and bad decisions. You can barely survive your last situationship. Forgetting is grace. But here's the good part: Your progress isn't erased. The instinct that stops you from doing something compulsive? That's wisdom earned in a body you've forgotten.

So, what's the grand purpose of all this?

The enlightened ones will tell you the rude truth: There isn't one. Life isn't a corporate ladder or a quest for meaning. You came from nothing, you'll return to nothing, and everything in between is the cosmic joke of consciousness pretending to be serious.

Life is an AR/VR game. You've got to realise it —and learn how to play it. Here's how it works:

Imagine a giant Ferris wheel. You start the cycle as a single-celled blob, just trying not to die. From then on, every action (Karma) you perform adds a little more data to your karmic hard drive. The more complex the data gets, the more complex your physical form becomes. You slowly graduate up the food chain—amoeba to amphibian, monkey to monk.

Apparently, after millions of births, you finally unlock the human version—the only creature capable of self-awareness. Till this point in the cycle, you've been adding karma on autopilot. But now, for the first time, you can consciously choose to start hitting 'delete' on the karmic mess you've accumulated and begin to descend the Ferris wheel.

That's why yogis say being human is not an accident—it's a privilege. Because for the first time, we get a say in our destiny. Every situation or person who triggers you is part of your karmic syllabus, designed to burn a portion of memory. And when you finally burn through it all—when there's nothing left to hold on to or identify with—your consciousness returns to where it began: Pure nothingness.

That's what the Hindus called *Moksha* and the Christians called 'Eternal Life'.

But why call it Eternal Life if you're technically dying and returning to no-thing?

Here's where the cosmic game gets even more interesting.

Just as human life moves in cycles, the universe itself runs on the same loop. There hasn't been one Big Bang—there have been many. According to Sadhguru, we're currently in the eighty-fourth Big Bang—which means eighty-three universes have already risen, evolved, and dissolved before this one. Each is a cosmic birth–death–rebirth cycle, like the inhale and exhale of creation itself.

The human design mirrors this cosmic rhythm. Yogic science tells us that we have 114 chakras—112 within the body and two beyond it. Going by this design, Sadhguru suggests that there will be 114 universal creations: 114 Big Bangs in total. The first 112 will belong to the realm of form—tangible matter, physical existence. The last two, 113 and 114, will exist beyond matter—pure consciousness, eternal and formless.

So, when a seeker says they want liberation, they're essentially saying: 'Fast-forward and take me to Level 114, where there is formless, eternal life—no suffering, no drama.'

Ultimately, if there is any purpose to life, it's this: To liberate yourself from the noise, the attachments, and the endless recycling of memory. To jailbreak your way out of illusion and return to the stillness from which you came.

Smoke & Mirrors

Seeing the design of the game doesn't mean you exit it overnight. It just means you become painfully aware you're still stuck on the ride. I mean, I had achieved near-sainthood levels of composure. Nothing could shake me—except one stubborn snag. A single, irritating thread still tethered me to Sankar, which was also somehow linked to my mother.

As the new year 2025 approached, I made myself a promise: Whatever was left, I'd burn it. So, I went nuclear. A seven-day water fast in Kerala, followed by twenty-one days of *Bhairavi Sadhana* and forty-two days of *Mahashivratri Sadhana*. No more half measures. Not just the masculine, not just the feminine—both, together.

My mother and sister decided to join me in Kerala because, apparently, the best place to confront your generational trauma is under the same roof as the people who caused it. I arrived calm, serene, radiating the smug glow of someone who thinks she's transcended family drama. That illusion lasted less than a day.

On day one, my mother slid into one of her classic self-pity spirals. It was ugly and desperate. A part of me knew she was holding up a mirror. The same way she couldn't let go of wanting my father's validation, I couldn't let go of wanting Sankar's. And I hated myself for it.

By day three without food, my inner saint had left the building, and my ugliest shadow stormed the stage. In a flash of pure reactivity, I punched my mother's left arm. She burst into tears—maybe from pain, maybe from shock, maybe because 'your child physically attacked you' is nowhere in the parenting manual.

The guilt hit instantly. I could've spiralled into self-loathing, but instead, I watched myself. I knew exactly what had happened: It was egoic, reactive, compulsive, and highly disrespectful.

And that's when I remembered the plate.

That crash was the soul's precision strike—it wasn't there to destroy, but to reveal. It was dharma in motion: Cool, conscious, corrective. This, however, was not. And it taught me the most uncomfortable lesson of all: There's a fire that purifies, and there is a fire that burns.

There's a dangerous high in discovering that rage can serve truth, but you have to know which kind you're channelling. One is a cosmic correction—born from clarity, anchored in awareness. The other is the ego's tantrum—born from pain, masked as righteousness.

Two weeks later, I was back in Coimbatore, deep in my sadhana and contemplating attending Sankar's show. That's when Yash appeared. With Sankar, I'd explored the feminine aspect. With Queen Bee, the masculine. And now, here came this man, right as I was bridging the two. It was as if the universe had been waiting for the exact moment I was finally balanced enough to face the final mirror. The timing of his arrival was impeccable.

From the beginning, there was a massive red flag. He spoke about the German woman with patriarchal nostalgia. He admired her love for his culture, her soft voice, and her covered head. He clearly wanted a woman who'd nurture his ego and never disagree. He expected love to make him feel good and be absolutely non-confrontational. But I walked in anyway—curious, like someone watching a predictable movie just to see how the disaster unfolds.

At first, he worshipped my insight. 'You're a healer,' he said once. 'I know you'll be the one to break through my walls.'

It felt divine. After years of being unseen by Sankar, finally, someone saw me. Besides, cohabiting with him was a dream—and he, too, admitted that he had never felt 'at home' the way he did at my place.

After he left, we were addicted to each other, unable to stop texting. I teased him in my best Yoda voice: 'Marry me, you will.' He laughed, but the joke stuck. Soon, it wasn't a joke—it was a hypothesis. He even said we'd make great babies. Match lit, both ends burning. A part of me saw his smug spiritual superiority and his ego's need to procreate. But I made it clear—it would only happen when and *if* we had *both* healed.

When work took me to his parents' city, he asked if I could meet them. His parents welcomed me like a long-lost relative. Even his brother came home mid-work to meet me. I felt as if I'd known them from another lifetime and probably liked them back then, too. I wasn't judging them, but I was observing. They were still very much subscribed to the unspoken rules of the matrix.

Yash, like most people, had grown up earning love through performance—good grades, good manners, good boy. Moreover, his brand of spirituality had convinced him that sexuality was dangerous and emotions were weaknesses to be 'transcended'. He treated feelings like clutter: The fewer you have, the more evolved you are. Which sounds profound—until you realise he was trying to fit a cathedral's worth of emotions into a broom cupboard.

And then, there I was—a cathedral of emotions with a philharmonic orchestra. I'd told him everything I saw, felt, envisioned, everything my higher self probably warned me not to say. My 'too-muchness' made him twitch. Vulnerable texts were met with emojis or silence.

Weeks into all this, he still hadn't told the German about me. When I confronted him, he said, 'I don't owe anyone explanations. I am not committed to anyone.' She was busy manifesting a life with him while he was discussing moving in with me. The sheer lack of integrity was shocking. And the fact that he saw nothing wrong was deeply disturbing.

When I started pointing out contradictions, he revoked. Every time I named a wound, he doubled down. 'I don't have any wounds,' he'd snap. 'You're getting hurt because of your own expectations.' When denial failed, he switched to gaslighting: 'It's all in your head. It's your truth. It's not the reality.' When that failed, he turned to spiritual bypassing: 'We are all flawed. Nobody is perfect.'

It was a maddening loop. I'd hand him the mirror, he'd smash it, and then claim the reflection never existed. He projected the same stuff, like someone had cloned Sankar, upgraded his body, and swapped alcohol for spirituality as his escape mechanism. Because make no mistake—Yash's 'yogi' life was just another form of running. He had mastered the fine art of weaponising his spirituality to dodge uncomfortable truths.

Suddenly, I was reminded of the time I had wished Sankar were even half as committed to the spiritual work as Yash. Turns out, commitment to a yoga routine is not a real commitment to growth. Avoidance is still avoidance, even when it chants *Aum*. In fact, I realised, it's worse when it hides behind enlightenment, because it calls disconnection 'detachment.'

The Sword of Clarity

The saviour complex I thought I'd buried with my family and Sankar came roaring back with Yash. Throughout my life, I had felt so unworthy that saving someone I loved seemed the surest path to redemption. And if there's one thing life keeps proving, it's that people don't get saved—they just drag their rescuers down with them.

Four months into our strange, undefined relationship, I flew to Rishikesh for his birthday, which happened to be in the same month as Sankar's, of course. I came armed with a suitcase full of gifts—the kind of gestures Sankar had never allowed. Yash met me with warmth that felt like a wish granted. Sankar never fed me, and Yash couldn't stop feeding me. For a moment, it felt as if the universe had righted a long-standing wrong.

It was all dreamy at first. But by day four, the cracks began to show. He was teaching a yoga session for his guests. Halfway through, I set the camera aside and joined in. Somewhere along the way, my body slipped into its own rhythm. Nobody seemed to mind—except him.

When the class ended, he humiliated me in front of everyone, as though I'd desecrated his holy altar by daring to be myself. His spiritual ego had taken a knock, and he stormed off in anger. I folded that red flag into a party hat and spent an hour pacifying him for one simple reason: I didn't want bad energy during his birthday week.

When we were finally physically intimate, it was unlike anything I had ever experienced. There was no performance; we simply rested in truth, holding each other until the dawn of his birthday, when a thunderstorm jolted us awake and we connected like a plug and socket. It wasn't sex in the usual sense, just stillness. He'd finally broken his five-year streak of celibacy.

The next day, a hailstorm rolled through. In a moment of playfulness, I sang a harmless tune, and he sneered, 'Your lesbian bug is still around.' My heart froze. In that one careless line, generations of inherited shame came spilling out. When I questioned him, he made his views clear: He didn't see fluidity as love; he saw it as a disease.

I tried to explain my experience of gender and love—how it wasn't about orientation but remembrance, recognising souls beyond their form. He nodded dismissively and offered an apology—the kind one gives merely to end a conversation.

Later that evening, I was in my room while he hid in the kitchen with his cook, texting passive-aggressively instead of coming to me directly. I stormed in and snapped at him, 'If you've got balls, come say it to my face.' His masculine pride couldn't bear that I'd questioned his balls in front of his staff. He retaliated with the worst of North Indian patriarchy—questioning my upbringing, my parents, and my decency: 'Women should behave. Women should know their place.'

The illusion had started to burn to ashes.

The next morning, we were supposed to meet his Guru in Haridwar. Before leaving, he said casually, 'If Guruji asks, don't mention that I drink or smoke.' This was his grand devotion? PR management? If he could lie to the one man he called his spiritual anchor, how much more was he lying to himself? The silence that followed was louder than the car engine carrying us there. I was simply observing it all, keenly.

His Guru was no fraud. He had real mastery. But his wound was visible—a deep ache for the recognition he had never received. Yash gave him unwavering importance, and in return, Yash basked in the glow of being singled out as the 'favourite disciple.' Suddenly, I saw the mirror his Guru was showing me, too.

At one point, we sat alone on the banks of the Ganga. I don't recall every word that passed between us, but I remember the texture of it—gaslighting, dismissal, distortion. Something in me snapped. The same cold, deliberate anger that once guided me to smash that plate returned. I pinned him down, looked him dead in the eye, took a deep breath and slapped him—once, cleanly.

When I released him, he came at me, clumsy and wild, like a classic wife-beater. When he was done thrashing me, I caught his collar, pulled him close, and screamed, 'Motherfucker!' so deep into his face it detonated the mother wound he had spent years pretending didn't exist. We wrestled, both possessed by something darker than us, until I finally shoved him into the Ganga.

I sank onto the steps, wounded and trembling, tears pouring down as he dragged himself out of the river, dripping. He sat beside me, water pooling at his feet, put his arm around me almost tenderly, and asked with genuine bewilderment, 'Where the hell did all that violence come from?'

And then, as if nothing had happened, he straightened his clothes and said, 'Wash your face before you come say goodbye to Guruji.' The fact that he cared more about the image of peace than peace itself was disorienting. But on the way back to the car, his question echoed: Where *did* that violence come from?

That's when a poem Queen Bee had written for me came flooding back—*Ganga*.

You are Ganga
as and when she comes out of Shiva's locks,
thunderous, carving her path,
uncaring about wreckage in her wake.

I am Ganga, too, but at Varanasi
filled with muck and corpses,
worshipped and abused in the same moment.

We are the same waters.
That's why we love each other.
But I can never come back to you,
and you can never reach me.

Being thrashed on the same river she'd written about, the penny finally dropped. Till then, I had cast her as the villain in my story—the vindictive woman out to punish the world for the violence she had endured. But sitting there, physically bruised, I finally saw the wound she was living from. I was her, and she was me.

I had never seen this brand of physical violence before. She had lived inside it for twelve years. Suddenly, her choices made sense—why she buried herself in work, why she refused alimony, why she wanted to play the saviour, why she cut people off so brutally.

The two acts of violence towards my mother—the plate and the punch—had taught me their difference: Violence born of ego corrodes; violence born of clarity liberates. I wasn't proud of slapping Yash, but I knew it was there to free us both. It wasn't pettiness. It was truth refusing to be silenced.

In a deranged way, Yash and I had both done each other a service. I had shown him that he isn't the saint he pretends to be. And he had knocked loose the resentment I'd been carrying towards Queen Bee. The universe, once again, played its joke with surgical precision.

DETACHMENT 101

Once I saw the design, I couldn't take it too personally. Sure, I was in shock at my bruises, but there was something liberating about it. The incident had cracked open years of resentment I didn't even know I was still carrying.

Yash, however, refused to see it that way. His illusion of being 'the good guy' had finally splintered. For the first time, he had a real chance to look at his shadows, to accept them, forgive himself, and maybe even love himself through them. Instead, he did what most people do when the mirror gets too bright—he turned it outward. He pinned the entire blame on me and continued to convince himself he was a saint.

He insisted his violence was justified because I had 'started it'. What he couldn't see was that I had merely responded to months of emotional and psychological warfare. It was like being slowly drowned and then blamed for wrestling my way up for air.

At first, I stooped to his level. I tried mirroring his tactics—sharp words, personal jabs—hoping he'd finally see what he was doing. But he was a professional deflector. He took the very behaviour meant to hold up the mirror and weaponised it against me. When that didn't work, I swung the other way—performing compassion, hoping that if I loved him enough, I'd melt the ice around his heart and help him love himself. But the more love I poured in, the more violent he became. It was like feeding a fire and praying it would cool down.

The intensity was too much, and we drifted apart for a bit. But signs, synchronicities, and that strange magnetic pull of karmic madness kept dragging us back together. I always told him we were Shiva-Shakti. Turns out, even the universe agreed. After one particularly bitter silence, he fell ill and was hospitalised. Talk about instant karma! I burst out laughing when he sent me a picture from the hospital. Above his bed hung a framed Shiva-Shakti yantra. Room number? 101. Lesson title: Shiva-Shakti 101. Even he couldn't ignore that syllabus.

Not long after, my divine travel agent, Prabhu, organised a trek near Bangalore—coincidentally, the same weekend Sankar was staging a play there. The universe had clearly scheduled a final exam. Without a second thought, I booked my ticket. I was finally ready—detached enough to attend his play in public without emotional fireworks.

When I got there, I felt nothing. No excitement, no nostalgia, not even the faintest romantic delusion. I watched half the play and left at the interval. It was the kindest thing I could do for myself—three and a half hours of classical Koodiyattam was well beyond my attention span. Not because I did not appreciate the art form, but because of the show's performative ego and refusal to adapt to a contemporary audience.

Besides, by leaving midway, I had also compassionately spared him the horror of seeing my face in the audience when he came to take a bow at the end.

I had passed the exam with flying colours. Sankar's spell had finally snapped. Fourteen years of karmic hypnosis—gone.

Back home, Yash and I tried again—another reboot, another promise to 'do the work'. But every time we reached any real depth, he'd retreat. Life kept handing him chances to step up: when my house help met with an accident, when I had to travel and needed someone to care for my pregnant cat, when I simply needed a partner who'd show up. Each time, he promised to come to Coimbatore. Each time, he flaked.

Yash's heart had glimpsed divine love, but his mind refused to trust it. The universe had delivered exactly what he'd been manifesting, but his awareness hadn't evolved enough to receive it. So, he projected his confusion onto me, and I became his punching bag.

Because he could not take responsibility for his actions, he blamed me for provocation.

Because he was ashamed of his own sexuality, he slut-shamed me.

Because he felt unworthy, he called me unattractive.

Because he couldn't accept his truth, he called me a liar.

Because he could not accept the significance of our connection, he mocked it.

Because he feared rejection, he rejected me first.

Because he felt weak in front of my strength, he kept breaking me.

Because he couldn't accept that he needed help, he called me crazy.

And somewhere along the way, I did start going crazy—apologising, shrinking, bowing, begging, explaining, justifying, holding space, bleeding empathy while my self-worth crumbled. He drove me so low that I found myself standing at the edge again—that dark, seductive whisper of suicide. It was hilarious, in a tragicomic way. Just when I thought I'd achieved *Zen*, the universe sent in Yash to test me.

But as Osho says, 'When you feel suicidal, it's not you who wants to die—it's your false self.' And I realised what was dying was my saviour complex. The part of me that believed I could heal someone who didn't want to heal. I didn't need to die; I just needed to stop trying to play God. That's when I directed myself to an institute for a series of formal psychological evaluations.

'Sane,' declared medical science—which was nice, considering the plotline. Despite falling apart so totally, I was declared sane! Having mastered my mind, the next thing on my list was my body. So, I signed up for Isha's *Angamardana* programme—mastery over the limbs.

For my whole life, my left knee had been my nemesis. I could never sit cross-legged, and I knew the block wasn't physical; it was karmic. Once, I'd even told Sankar, 'You're going to help me release this block.' And every time my knee refused to bend the way I needed it to, I'd secretly think that maybe it just needed to break so it could be rebuilt.

Here's the cosmic joke: just as I released Yash and chose to reclaim my life, it happened. On the second day of Angamardana, in front of a photo of Sadhguru, during one intense movement, my knee snapped. Clean. The karmic knot had finally popped.

Surgery followed, and I was alone in Coimbatore with four cats to care for.

Yash had once promised me at the start of our relationship, 'I don't know about anything else. But if you ever find yourself in difficult times and there's no one, I will be there.'

The universe had given him one last chance to step up. He said he wanted to. And then, after a warm, vulnerable conversation one day, his switch flipped—again. Without any consideration for the state I was in, he pushed me away.

That was the end of the illusion. By this time, I could take nothing personally or seriously. Not my injury. Not his behaviour. Not even my pain. So, I just laughed.

He always blamed timing for his avoidance. 'The time isn't right,' he'd say. 'The time will come.'

It reminded me of something my maths tutor used to say every time he caught a student staring at the clock instead of paying attention to the problem: 'Time will pass,' he used to say, 'You may not.' And so, while Yash waited for time to pass, I decided to pass through time.

Natural Selection 2.0

Destiny is the Prarabdha Karma we're born with. Free will is what we make of it—the highest possibility we carve out of the chaos.

Every few decades, life hands us personal upgrade packages. At thirty-three and sixty, the solar return cycles roll around, hitting refresh on our purpose and priorities. But beyond these personal checkpoints, there are larger cosmic rhythms at play: cycles that don't just reboot individuals but reset the consciousness of entire species.

The ancients called them *Yugas*—vast epochs through which human awareness rises, falls, and rises again. Yogic sciences describe that, just as the Earth orbits the Sun, our entire solar system moves in an elliptical dance with another mysterious star that science is yet to discover.

When our solar system swings closer to this Supersun, the Ether—the fifth element that governs communication and perception—grows dense. Awareness heightens, truth becomes self-evident, and human consciousness operates like high-speed Wi-Fi. But as we drift away, the signal weakens. Misunderstandings multiply, truth gets lost in translation, and humanity starts bickering about whose God has the better marketing team.

Traditional pundits may debate the numbers, but sages like Shri Yukteshwar and Sadhguru, who read time through awareness rather than scripture, offer a timeline that makes startling sense:

1. **Sat Yuga (Golden Age):** 5,184 years of clarity and communion with the divine.
2. **Treta Yuga (Silver Age):** 3,888 years of virtue and order.
3. **Dwapara Yuga (Bronze Age):** 2,592 years of duality and discovery.
4. **Kali Yuga (Iron Age):** 1,296 years of confusion, conflict, and collapse.

Together, they form one *Mahayuga*, a 25,920-year cycle—a cosmic breath where half is the descent into darkness and the other half, the climb back to light.

The Mahabharata marked the start of the Kali Yuga roughly 5,000 years ago, which means we've already crossed the basement and are ascending again. Right now, humanity is in the final stretch of Dwapara Yuga, inching toward Treta, the Silver Age. According to Sadhguru, by around 2082, we'll complete that transition.

The rise in our ability to communicate is evident. In just a few centuries, we've gone from fire to fibre optics, from decoding atoms to creating artificial intelligence. We can speak across continents, merge human and machine, and livestream our meditations. Yes, the world looks chaotic, but consciousness is expanding. Technology is the mirror, reflecting the subtle intelligence awakening within us.

And that brings us to what I call 'Natural Selection 2.0.'

Once upon a Darwin, survival favoured the fittest—the strongest, fastest, and most adaptable. But the rules have changed. Machines have taken all the medals for muscle, speed, and IQ. The only thing left they can't replicate is consciousness: Emotion, empathy, intuition, and presence.

In this new evolutionary game, survival won't depend on biceps or bank accounts; it'll depend on bandwidth. Because the next leap in evolution isn't physical—it's spiritual.

And the split is already showing. People who can't regulate their emotions are burning out. Those clinging to rage, greed, and fear are collapsing under the density of their own vibration. Meanwhile, the ones who can breathe through chaos, transmute pain into awareness, and stay grounded in compassion—they're not just surviving; they're thriving.

COVID was the first elimination round. And the irony is that stress and fear took down more people than the virus ever could. Science looked for mutations in cells, but the real mutation was energetic. Those who could turn panic into presence, loneliness into introspection, and mortality into meaning became immune in ways no vaccine could promise.

The Earth isn't filtering for strong bodies anymore; it's filtering for awake minds. It's filtering for those willing to do the inner work.

But awakening, too, comes with its own fine print. The moment you stumble upon even a spark of light, the ego sneaks back in through the side door—this time wearing a halo. The same part of you that once wanted to be admired for your looks or achievements now wants to be adored for your wisdom or ability to save others. 'If I can't be loved,' it whispers, 'let me at least be useful.'

The need to be 'somebody' doesn't disappear; it just gets a rebrand. Helping becomes the new high. And like all highs, it starts pure: you've suffered, you've alchemised, and now you want to spare others the same pain. But here's the catch: trying to save people from their own karma isn't compassion; it's interference. And every time you try to pull someone out of their darkness before they've learnt to see in it, you rob them of the very wisdom they came here to earn.

The more you interfere, the more you entangle yourself.

DIVINE DUTY

Let's talk about what actually happens when you 'heal' someone—and why rushing to become a healer before you've fully healed yourself can be hazardous to your health.

Every human being emits an electromagnetic field that mirrors their emotional state. When a healer enters another person's field, their nervous system acts like a tuning fork. Through resonance and mirror neurons, the healer begins vibrating at the same frequency as the one they're helping—grief, shame, anxiety, whatever flavour of suffering's on the menu.

But instead of recoiling, the healer stabilises that frequency, transmuting it through love, compassion, and neutrality. Think of it as emotional osmosis: Their darkness crosses your membrane of light until equilibrium is restored.

In spiritual terms, this is what happens when evolved beings or gurus 'take on' karma. It's not a poetic metaphor—it's literal energetic composting. The guru's body becomes a recycling bin for humanity's unresolved muck. The more they give, the more sludge flows through their own system.

You've probably noticed that many saints and mystics didn't exactly retire on a beach with a glow-up and a coconut. Ramakrishna died of throat cancer. Ramana Maharshi of Sarcoma. Yogananda's body deteriorated rapidly. Sadhguru just survived a brain bleed. Even Jesus wasn't spared the crucifixion clause.

To the casual cynic, that looks like failure. 'If you're so enlightened, why the pain?' But that's the misunderstanding. Enlightenment isn't immunity; it's willingness.

For them, it isn't suffering—it's service. A guru's illness is humanity detoxing through their body. They don't resist it because they no longer see separation between 'my body' and 'the collective.' When they cough, the world exhales.

That's what 'Jesus died for your sins' really meant. He didn't die because of sin—he died into it. He absorbed collective unconsciousness, alchemised it through love, and showed us what happens when divinity refuses to flinch before human darkness.

But here's the catch: Most of us aren't Jesus. Or Ramakrishna. Or Sadhguru. We're interns at best—still figuring out which end of the incense stick to light.

You get one glimpse of transcendence, heal your inner child, start seeing angel numbers on speed dial, and suddenly you're like, 'Come, sign up for my retreat!' This is the sneakiest phase of awakening. You've barely scrubbed your own karmic toilet, and already you're handing out toilet brushes.

The universe will correct that delusion gently—usually in the form of energetic burnout. You start absorbing other people's density like a psychic sponge. Their depression becomes your exhaustion, their chaos your confusion, their heartbreak your mysterious back pain. Before you know it, you're sitting in bed with a Himalayan salt lamp, wondering why the healer needs healing again.

Because it wasn't dharma. It was a trauma response, wearing a white robe.

Dharma doesn't arise from the need to be needed. It arises when even that need dissolves. True service is silent, invisible, effortless. It doesn't drain you—it flows through you, like breath. That's why great masters could carry the karmas of millions without complaint. They didn't take it on; they let it pass through.

When Ramakrishna or Jesus or Sadhguru experienced physical suffering, they weren't punished. They had simply become so vast, so porous, that the collective could detox through them without leaving a trace of 'me.' They didn't flinch because they'd already died before dying—the ego was long gone.

The final stage of awakening is when you stop being the hero and start being the hollow reed through which consciousness can flow.

Finding your dharma feels less like a discovery and more like a death. The ego dies, and in its funeral pyre, you're reminded of your role in the play. It's the moment you stop asking, 'What's my passion? What's my purpose?' and realise that you're simply here to do what is needed. Your work neither gives you satisfaction, nor does it give you misery.

You start noticing patterns that were always there—your obsessions, your heartbreaks, your random talents—all converging into a single thread of service. You see how the universe has been subtly grooming you for this role. When you're aligned with dharma, your body becomes its instrument.

At some point, the soul starts whispering the one direction no one wants to hear: You're not here to be loved. You're here to serve.

Most people cannot digest that. Because who in their right mind wants to go from main character to maintenance worker in God's cosmic janitorial department? But that's the quiet truth of dharma. When the need to be 'somebody' dissolves—when applause, validation, spiritual ambition, and the desperate hope that someone will finally see how 'special' you are dissolves—what's left is, finally, freedom.

MUKTI: THE ULTIMATE LIBERATION

All my life, the men I loved ghosted me. They left when things got real, when feelings got messy, when honesty got uncomfortable. And then came Yash—the one who did not. He stayed through every argument and replied to every message. Not to love me, but to show me what love is not.

Through him, I finally understood what Sankar had been trying to teach me all along. The silence, the absence, and the avoidance were not punishments; they were mirrors, reflecting my own habit of running from evolution by clinging to pain and trying to fix everyone to prove my worth. Yash stayed so I could finally stop running. He taught me that walking away isn't always an act of ego or fear. Sometimes, it is love in its highest form. The kind that comes with clarity, compassion, and calm.

I didn't have the heart to block him. That felt too abrupt for something that had once held so much weight in my life. Instead, I kept telling him, over and over again, that I was done. Eventually, out of his own fear of abandonment, he blocked me. There was something strangely fitting about that ending. For once, I wasn't the one being left. I had already chosen to leave, even if I hadn't physically enacted it.

I won't lie. The temptation to reach out to him didn't magically disappear. It sat there like a bad habit that didn't get the memo that we've evolved. Some days, it was loud; some days, it was just a quiet itch. But for once, I didn't act on it. Not because I was trying to prove a point or being 'strong', but because something in me had finally understood that choosing myself isn't a one-time declaration. It's a daily, slightly boring, and slightly uncomfortable practice.

So, I stayed with myself. I showed up. I wrote. I finished this book.

If you're reading this sub-chapter, what you're holding is not the original version. It's a reprint. The first version was released on Mahashivratri 2026, after what felt like an unnecessarily long series of delays at the press. In hindsight, the timing was just doing what timing does best—ignoring your plans and sticking to its own.

As the week after its release on Shiva's day, something bizarre started happening.

People began messaging me, saying their books were falling apart. Pages literally slipping out. Bindings giving up. Entire sections detaching like the book had commitment issues. According to the publisher, this had never happened before. Not once. In all their years. Which, in my experience, is usually the universe's favourite opening line before it does something very on brand.

Now, by this point, my brain had stopped accepting 'random' as an explanation for anything. So, while everyone else was looking at it as a production defect, I was sitting there thinking, 'Okay, universe . . . what are you trying to say?'

I just didn't know the answer yet.

In the midst of all this, my family came down to Coimbatore, and we drove over to Kerala for a *Kalasarpa Shanti* ritual. In simple terms, it's a ritual meant to address the Rahu-Ketu (North-South Lunar

Nodes) axis—the part of your karmic blueprint that governs your past tendencies and your future direction.

Something about that whole experience settled me. Then, on the drive back home, after dropping my family at the airport, I felt an unexpected urge to call Yash. Not in the usual 'I miss him' way. It was strange. I wasn't yearning. I wasn't emotional. I just had this excess energy, like something had shifted in me and needed somewhere to go.

Unlike Sankar, who treated my calls like spam, Yash picked up almost instantly. There was a warmth in his voice that caught me off guard, not the kind that tries to impress or smooth things over, but something simpler, more present. It felt easy, like we hadn't spent months not speaking, as if nothing had calcified in the space between us.

The first thing he said was, 'If you hadn't called me, I was going to reach out to you in a few days.' And I remember noticing the absence of tension in myself as he said it. No suspicion, no need to decode, no mental gymnastics trying to figure out what he meant. Just a quiet recognition. This is what resonance feels like when it isn't being forced into existence.

What followed was one of the most honest conversations we had ever had. There was no defensiveness creeping in through the back door, no subtle shifting of blame, no attempt to control the narrative. It was simply two people speaking, listening, and responding without the usual undercurrents of distortion. For the first time, it felt like we were not trying to win or guard anything, just trying to understand.

In the months that we had not spoken, life had clearly stepped in and taken over the role I had been so determined to play. He told me he had landed in the ICU and then back in a hospital room numbered 101, which—at this point—felt like the universe was making sure the message was impossible to ignore.

It became obvious, in a way that didn't need to be stated, that something had shifted in him during that time. Life had taught him what I had spent months trying and failing to explain. And there was a certain humility in that realisation, at least on my end. When I stopped trying to save him, he had found a way to meet himself.

Over the next few days, we continued speaking in long, unguarded conversations. We spoke about everything that had happened between us, the patterns we had both fallen into, how we had hurt each other, and for the first time, there was no attempt to minimise or justify any of it.

His apologies didn't feel like tools to restore access; they felt like acknowledgements that didn't need anything in return. There was effort, there was consistency, and there was a kind of care that didn't disappear the moment things became difficult. His love didn't feel like something I had to fight for or extract. It was simply there.

For the first time in my life, I felt safe, not because someone was finally doing all the right things, but because I was no longer abandoning myself in the process of being with them. That constant internal negotiation, the one where I would override my own instincts to maintain connection, was no longer running the show.

I don't know what this relationship will become, and for once, that doesn't feel like a problem to solve. However, if I am being completely honest, of course, there is a quiet knowing within me. But I have finally learnt that knowing does not need to be turned into control. It does not need to be rushed into form before it is ready.

What feels clear, however, is something far simpler: Neither of us is going to abandon the other in the ways that actually matter. Not through avoidance, not through distortion, not through the subtle ways in which people disappear while still technically being present.

And having seen each other at our worst, having gone through our most difficult phases without depending on each other to hold us together, whatever exists between us now is not rooted in need or codependency. There is no saviour dynamic left to play out, no quiet expectation that the other person will fix what we have not yet faced within ourselves.

There is just a willingness to show up, as we are, and let that be enough.

Finally, the binding incident with the book began to make sense. The story had truth, it had insight, it had dismantling, but it did not yet have the one thing that allows all of that to hold together without collapsing under its own weight: Hope. Not as a fairy tale or a perfect ending, but a sense that all this heartbreaking, gut-wrenching inner work leads somewhere.

Because it does.

Nothing in this story is accidental. Not the people who entered, not the ways in which they left, not the timing of what broke and what returned, not even the book quite literally coming apart at the seams. What once felt like chaos, like a series of disconnected events, now reveals itself as something far more structured and intentional, becoming visible only in hindsight.

Finally, there is also the poetic artistry of the Source of Creation: If Sankar means 'Lord of Destruction', Yash means 'Victory'.

Solulu 8

Save Yourself First

99 per cent of human effort to 'fix the world' comes from insecurity—the aching belief that if we can just heal someone, fix something, or make the world a little better, then maybe we'll finally matter. It looks noble, but it's really the adult costume of a wounded child who couldn't save her parents, her lover, or her past self.

When you rush to save, you unknowingly step onto a pedestal. You tell yourself you're helping, but what you're really saying is, 'I know better.' And the moment you put yourself above someone, you take their power away. They were already feeling weak, and now you've made them feel weaker instead of more empowered. That's why they retaliate—through shutdown, silence, anger, or violence.

Most of what we call service isn't compassion; it's a trauma response. Everyone has a right to their pain. Suffering isn't punishment: It's the syllabus of the soul. When you interrupt it, you're basically hacking into their divine curriculum because you can't bear to watch them fall. So, you scoop up their lessons, carry their pain, and then wonder why your back hurts.

Eventually, the universe steps in to correct the delusion until you finally understand the difference between service and self-sacrifice. Self-sacrifice drains—you collapse after, you keep score, you crave validation. Service flows—you're energised, detached, unbothered by credit. You could disappear, and the work would continue.

But even awakening has its traps. Once you outgrow the saviour complex, the ego simply rebrands. Now you're a healer, a starseed, a lightworker, a way-shower. You've swapped your corporate badge for cosmic credentials. But the addiction is the same—the need to feel special. The moment you feel 'chosen', you've missed the point. Enlightenment was never meant to make you extraordinary; it was meant to make you *extra*ordinary.

There's nothing wrong with the labels—they serve a purpose. Call yourself whatever helps you do your work. Just make sure the label remains functional, not hierarchical. Because the second you start feeling satisfaction in your service, the ego has snuck back in. If your work as a healer makes you feel 'good', it's not service yet. True service neither uplifts nor exhausts you—it simply moves through you. Like breath. Silent, invisible, and necessary.

Ultimately, you can't save anyone. You can only remind them of their own capacity to save themselves. Just like a real guru doesn't fix you—they hold a frequency where self-healing becomes inevitable. That's the essence of love, too: It doesn't carry you; it stands beside you until you remember how to walk.

When you finally stop meddling, the world begins to heal itself. The trees still grow. The oceans still breathe. People still make the same mistakes—and still wake up anyway.

That's the final initiation—not martyrdom, not sainthood, but humility. The willingness to be ordinary in the service of something extraordinary.

To love without an agenda and to create without an audience.

EPILOGUE

'When the soul is ready,

its words come through like floodwater.'

- Khalil Gibran

All my life, I doubted my writing. So, it's almost poetic that this book wasn't born out of ambition. It was born the day I stopped trying to be somebody and accidentally became a nobody.

One quiet morning, I went for a bicycle ride, sat by a lake, and started typing whatever poured through me. No filters, no outline, no purpose. I sent those few pages to my family WhatsApp group and told them, 'I think I'm being called to write a book.'

Here's the magical part: A few days prior, Hay House had reached out to my sister to explore book ideas. She didn't have one. I did. So, I sent them a sample—just a few unpolished pages from that lakeside download. They read it, liked it, and just like that, I effortlessly had a publisher.

The writing that followed was an exorcism. Every time I tried to finish a chapter, life would hand me a new one. Deadlines collapsed because my writing blocks turned out to be spiritual roadblocks in disguise. Each time, I'd message my editor saying, 'I'm delayed again,' only to realise the story I was writing hadn't finished happening. The lessons I was writing about were unfolding in real time.

For months, I chased Sankar for a reflection of what I was missing. I wanted him to show me what I couldn't see in myself so I could write it out of my system. When he disappeared, the universe sent Yash—same mirror, new frame. Between the two of them, every unfinished sentence in me found its full stop.

And then there was the timing—so absurdly perfect. After all the delays, rewrites, and breakdowns, I finished this manuscript exactly on the day of Diwali, 2025. Diwali marks Ram's return from fourteen years of exile. And 2025 marked fourteen years since my saga with Sankar began.

Every single 'solulu' in this book isn't a theory; it's something I have lived, bled for, and occasionally cursed and wailed my way through. And if anything in these pages resonates, it's because it's forged, not fabricated.

I didn't write this book to be a bestseller. Honestly, I didn't even write it to sell. I wrote it because it wouldn't stop writing itself through me. Because somewhere between heartbreak and healing, it became clear that this right here was my Dharma.

What you do with it now is yours. Like it, love it, judge it, mock it, accept it, reject it—it doesn't matter.

My karma was to write it. Yours is to meet it however you're meant to.

कर्मण्येवाधिकारस्ते मा फलेषु कदाचन।
मा कर्मफलहेतुर्भूर्मा ते संगोऽस्त्वकर्मणि॥

Karmanye vādhikaraste mā phaleshu kadachana,
Mā karmaphalaheturbhurma te sango'stvakarmani.

You have the right to perform your actions,
but never to the fruits of those actions.
Let not the results of your work be your motive,
nor let your attachment be to inaction.

ACKNOWLEDGEMENTS

'We are all just walking each other home.'

– Ram Dass

To my parents, Vipul and Purnima. Thank you for planting the seed of liberation in me and somehow managing to nurture it while questioning every decision I've ever made. You've shown me that growth doesn't end with parenthood and that it's never too late to learn. Your resilience, humour, courage, generosity, willingness to evolve, and ability to love unconditionally have shaped me more than you know.

To my sister, Rytasha. Thank you for calling me out on all my bullshit and being the only person who truly saw through all of me. You've questioned my life choices with such flair that it deserves an award. But through it all, you've been my greatest fan and loudest cheerleader.

To my paternal grandmother, Kalavati, my maternal grandfather, Champaklal, and my aunts Dharmisthaa and Bina, for your unwavering love, acceptance and support through the most questionable phases of my life.

To my teachers, Sister Babitha, Bipin, and Gisli, who touched my life in ways that will echo forever. You held space for me to grow when I didn't yet know how.

To my friends, especially Ajay, Amalina, Arsheen, Chi, Dhanalakshmi, Dhawalika, Dimitri, Gauri, Gayatri, Henna, Kulsum, Lilya, Maleesha, Mathis, Prabhu, Prashant, Prithvi, Rehina, Richa, Rudra, Sahar, Simi, Sonia, Swami Patanga, Zohra, and Zoya. Your presence brought me the safest energy I've ever known. Thank you for orbiting my world.

To Bilaroo, Meow, Nara, and Simha. Thank you for the purrs, the cuddles, and the reminder that, sometimes, lying in a sunbeam is enough.

To Mister Mirage, Queen Bee, Ziad, and every other emotionally unavailable person I've fancied. Thank you for the love and the pain that cracked me open. Your presence and absence were the most powerful teachers of my life.

To the only man I have ever truly loved, Sankar Venkateswaran and Yash Maini. I see no separation between you—or between us. Through you, I learnt that love is not two becoming one, but one remembering itself through two. Thank you for being the mirror through which I realised myself.

To Sadhguru. Thank you for being the best GPS any seeker could ask for. Even when I lost signal, took twelve detours, and loudly questioned the whole route, your grace kept pulling me back. Through Inner Engineering, I learnt to engineer my mental health. This book, in its deepest truth, is an offering to you.

And lastly, I thank Me.

For letting pain make me wise instead of wounded.

For refusing to let others' projections define my worth.

For holding my own hand when no one else could.

For asking for help, even when pride whispered not to.

For choosing softness, even when hardness promised an easier survival.

For choosing truth over image, even when it cost me comfort, belonging and love.

For surrendering to life—without needing to be right, seen or understood.

'The gateways to wisdom and knowledge are always open.'

Louise Hay